44.

45. # THE

46. # BORDERLINE

47. # PERSONALITY

48. # DISORDER

49. # WELLNESS

50. # PLANNER

51. # FOR FAMILIES

52. **52** weeks of hope, inspiration, and mindful ideas for greater peace and happiness

Amanda L. Smith, LCSW
Foreword by Perry Hoffman, PhD

UNHOOKED BOOKS
An Imprint of High Conflict Institute Press
Scottsdale, Arizona

© 2018 by Amanda L. Smith

Unhooked Books, LLC
7701 E. Indian School Rd., Ste. F
Scottsdale, AZ 85251
www.unhookedbooks.com

ISBN: 978-1-936268-29-0

Library of Congress Control Number: 2018933277

Design by Julian Leon, The Missive (www.themissive.com)

CONTENTS

FOREWORD

BY PERRY HOFFMAN, PHD

It is both a personal and professional honor for me to write the foreword to *The Borderline Personality Disorder Wellness Planner*. Meeting Amanda a number of years ago through the organization she created in Florida, I was immediately impressed. Florida Borderline Personality Disorder Association was a landmark accomplishment. To my knowledge, it was the first-ever individual state effort for borderline personality disorder (BPD) and it developed a reputation of national recognition.

The *Borderline Personality Disorder Wellness Planner* is another unique effort and Amanda has once again has created a wonderful resource. This time a resource specifically for families with a loved one with BPD, the planner offers an opportunity to learn skills while at the same time providing a forum for self-care assessment along with skill acquisition and application.

Based on Dialectical Behavior Therapy (DBT), each page introduces a skill that promotes management of one's emotions and life in more effective ways.

DBT skills are well-documented for the individual with BPD and also have been shown to be a good match for families as well. As the first person to teach DBT skills to families, I saw first hand the changes that were effected from even the initial class meeting (Linehan, 1993, page 37). This planner expands that effort by organizing both skill exposure and self-care assessments into a well-needed, systematic and effective 52 -week program.

Why is a focus on family important? BPD is a disorder that centers on relationships with seven of its nine symptoms having interpersonal impact. In addition, research showed that emotional involvement with the loved one promotes their recovery. Other data looked at the disorder from a different perspective and documented that over 53% of family members met criteria for post traumatic stress disorder based only on witnessing and experiencing their loved one's BPD symptoms. Experiencing high personal stress as a consequence compromises the family member's resilience both emotionally and physically.

Still a very underserved and misunderstood part of the BPD community, the journey of families is a challenging one with highs and lows on any given day. Amanda has conveyed a compassionate understanding and respect for the families on her website and now through the *Wellness Planner*. Historically that was not the common sentiment. Families were not considered partners in the recovery process. However, in the past decade the tide has fortunately changed and Amanda has devoted time and energy to contribute to that effort. Her message of empathy along with a consistent message of caring and concern both for the sufferer and their relatives has further promoted the needs and rights of family members.

Amanda illustrates the importance of a dialectical perspective not forgetting that the person in recovery is central and yet at the same time that family member needs cannot be ignored. As with professionals, family members also need tools for both their own well-being and also to be able to be a valued resource for their relative. Amanda's innovative way of recognizing families with the planner promotes that importance.

Bravo!

Perry D. Hoffman, PhD
President and co-founder
National Education Alliance for
Borderline Personality Disorder
Co-creator Family Connections™ Program
www.borderlinepersonalitydisorder.com

DEDICATION
TO DAVID. THANK YOU FOR BEING
A PART OF MY LIFE WORTH LIVING.

PREFACE

I've been truly honored to personally work or consult with individuals diagnosed with Borderline Personality Disorder (BPD) and their families for over a decade now. I've spoken with people throughout the United States and around the world in an effort to help them get the treatment they are seeking.

I really love my therapy and family consultation practice and have found so much inspiration from the many clients who have trusted me enough to help them on their journey toward feeling better.

Throughout this book, I sometimes share stories collected over many years as a way to help illustrate common pitfalls families sometimes experience or the effective steps families are often taking. Any names, details, and circumstances of individuals mentioned in this book have been changed to protect the privacy of family members and friends who are doing their very best while enduring daily challenges. It is important to recognize that families coping with a mental health diagnosis share similar struggles wherever they live.

Often there is a loneliness or isolation for families that follows a diagnosis of BPD; however, you are not alone. I hope that this book helps you to see that your own personal story is not all that different from the experiences of thousands of individuals I've spoken with or heard from throughout the years.

The ideas and techniques found on the pages within this book come from evidence-based treatment approaches that have been tried and tested in peer-reviewed research. As an intensively-trained DBT therapist, I've borrowed some ideas from Dialectical Behavior Therapy (DBT) but also from another approach I love called Mentalization-Based Treatment (MBT). Other information is based on research about the effectiveness of mindfulness and self-compassion practices. Because these ideas may be new to you, I encourage you keep an open mind while reading.

Finally, this book is not intended as a substitute for excellent health care with a trained professional. In the resource section of this book, I have recommendations for locating well-qualified professionals who specialize in the treatment of BPD.

Above all else, don't give up.

Amanda L. Smith, LCSW
hopeforbpd.com

START HERE

Today is a new day. This is your day.
If you are holding this book in your hands, please know that I'm already a fan of yours.

I started this work over a decade ago, and I firmly believe that I have worked with some of the best families in the world: families who are dedicated, loyal, compassionate, and consistently hopeful that the future for their loved one will be brighter. Over the years, I've witnessed those changed lives in my own practice. I love watching clients reach their goals. I've seen them complete school and go to work. I've also seen clients get married and start families of their own. There are so many reasons for family members to anticipate success.

MY HOPE IS THAT USING THIS BOOK WEEK AFTER WEEK WILL HELP YOU TO:

Take care of yourself
so that you can
take care of those individuals you love so much.

Throughout the next 52 weeks, I want for you to remember that even people who are suffering from emotional pain and who are engaging in self-sabotaging behaviors get better, recover, and go on to create meaningful lives.

We know that people get better with specific treatments (referred to as evidence-based treatment in this book) designed to target the symptoms related to BPD. These treatments include Dialectical Behavior Therapy, Mentalization-Based Treatment, Transference-Focused Psychotherapy, Schema Therapy, STEPPS, and Good Psychiatric Management. We also know that family involvement and support make treatment outcomes even better. When I see families working together, I get really excited. Again and again, I've seen the difference it makes.

It doesn't matter if you are a spouse, mom, dad, sister, aunt, grandparent, boyfriend, or even a best friend. Whoever you are, congratulations. You are in the perfect place to make a lasting difference in your loved one's life. You can be a role model, a cheerleader, and an essential resource for information about recovery from BPD.

I want for you to believe in recovery. I want for you to believe in change. I want for you to believe that a year from now things can be different. Even if treatment has failed in the past, there are still reasons for you to be hopeful about the future.

GETTING TREATMENT

I want for your loved one to have a well-trained therapist and be involved with a strong treatment program. Because I wish for your family member to get the best in care, I've listed below several guidelines for finding a therapist or treatment programs.

1. Look for a therapist who specializes in an evidenced-based treatment for BPD. That means that they'll have specific training in a treatment that was designed to help individuals with BPD.

   Reading a few books or attending a weekend workshop does not prepare any therapist for working with individuals with BPD.

   Family members have a responsibility to ask the question, "Tell me about your training. Who did you train with?" or "What kind of training have you been a part of over the previous two years?"

2. Ask the therapist why they enjoy working with individuals with BPD. The best therapists are the ones who love their work. Understanding their "why" may help you to assess a good fit.

3. You can also ask about how the treatment is structured. For instance, DBT will look different from Transference-Focused Psychotherapy. Good Psychiatric Management will also look very different from STEPPS.

   Knowing what to expect in treatment or taking the time to learn more about a particular treatment will be very important for most families.

4. Unfortunately, evidence-based treatment isn't always affordable or even available. In areas of the world where there may be fewer treatment options, families may decide to accept that they are doing their very best with what they have available rather than giving up.

At the back of this book, you'll find even more resources for getting the help you need, but if you get stuck, reach out to me at amanda@hopeforbpd.com. I want to hear from you.

A FINAL WORD

Before you dive into the first week, I want to urge you to think about two ideas that will also help you over the **next 52 weeks:** patience and self-compassion.

I WANT FOR YOU TO HAVE PATIENCE WITH YOURSELF,

Patience with others, and also patience in a world where help for BPD isn't always as accessible as we'd like. Giving up is never the answer. Saying, "Let's keep looking. Let's have faith that we'll figure this out." will help keep you and your family member on the right path.

Sometimes all it takes is one more phone call or one more email to find the help we've been seeking.

SELF-COMPASSION IS ALSO IMPORTANT.

Along the way, you'll invariably make a mistake (or maybe many), or you may say something you wish you hadn't said in a moment of anger or fear. A commitment to self-compassion will allow you to treat yourself with kindness and keep going. If you become discouraged, others will follow.

Self-compassion will help you to stay the course throughout this adventure.

HOW TO USE THIS WELLNESS PLANNER

While there is no perfect way to use this planner, I'd encourage you to take it week by week.

It's tempting to think that we can get all of the information we need in a short amount of time and then be able to quickly use what we've learned to help ourselves and those we care about. Most of the time, however, significant improvement in behavior will take place over a period of months and years— not days or weeks. This is your reminder to be patient with yourself and your family member.

My hope is that over the next 52 weeks you'll begin to see a pattern of little changes that make a big difference in how you feel.

Please also remember to celebrate your small successes. This is exceptionally important work that you're doing for yourself.

BE BRAVE AS YOU MOVE FORWARD!

FIRST
Complete the Self-Care Assessment on pages 14–15

WEEKLY
Turn to the following page and start using the Weekly Self-Care Tracker during the week.

MONTHLY
Complete the Self-Care Assessment every four weeks.

YOUR WEEKLY WELLNESS PLANNER

MONTHLY
SELF-CARE ASSESSMENT

Over the past 28 days, how often have you engaged in these specific self-care methods?

PHYSICAL CARE	SCORE
Exercised 4-6 times a week	
Balanced sleep	
Paid attention to nutrition	
Ate mindfully	
Used alcohol in moderation	
Did not self-medicate	

TOTAL SCORE FOR THIS SECTION

EMOTIONAL CARE	SCORE
Asked for help	
Went to individual or family therapy	
Made time for enjoyable activities	
Practiced self-compassion	
Engaged in pleasurable activities and hobbies	
Sought meaning and purpose in my life	

TOTAL SCORE FOR THIS SECTION

TOTAL SCORE PER SECTION

20-24	**Excellent!** You're doing a great job of taking care of yourself in this area.
15-19	**Very good.** Identify and address any gaps in self-care.
BELOW 15	**No one is perfect.** Is this an area of growth for you?

Remember, a score of zero (not applicable) in any area may lower your section score.

RELATIONAL CARE	SCORE
Told people close to me why they were important	
Established or maintained healthy limits when necessary	
Let go of being "right"	
Took a nonjudgmental stance toward others	
Practiced empathy	
Spent time with people I care about	

TOTAL SCORE FOR THIS SECTION

SPIRITUAL CARE	SCORE
Attended religious or spiritual services	
Spent time with others who have similar beliefs and goals	
Practiced mindfulness or meditated	
Prayed or asked others to pray for me	
Read or watched things that inspire me	
Honored my own values	

TOTAL SCORE FOR THIS SECTION

YOU ARE NOT ALONE

Although I've been involved in advocacy and educational work for many years now, I must admit that there was a time early on when it came as a surprise to realize that **any kind of mental health diagnosis really does affect the entire family.**

It's never just the individual with BPD who suffers. That is not something I fully understood until I started speaking with parents, spouses, siblings, and friends.

So years ago I wasn't prepared when a mom told me that she calls 9-1-1 once a month or so when her daughter is in crisis. She let me know that she wasn't afraid that the daughter would hurt herself or someone else but that the only time she was able to get a good night's sleep was when her daughter was in the hospital and the home was peacefully and temporarily quiet.

I also wasn't ready for a confession from the dad who called me and admitted that he had abused his daughter and desperately wanted for her to get help so that the family legacy of mental illness, addiction, and physical abuse wouldn't continue for another generation.

I didn't know what to say when, at a local mental health support group, a mom confided that there were times when she hoped that the next suicide attempt her daughter made was successful because everyone in the family had been hurting for far too long. The stress they were living under led her to think about suicide more than once.

And today? Today I'm not surprised when a consulting client tells me that she had to drop out of the family psychoeducation class she was excited about attending because she recognizes that she needs treatment before she can be there for her son.

BPD is a family problem. We might want to insist that only one person needs help but the truth is that almost everyone could probably benefit from some extra support, guidance, education, and help with problem-solving our toughest issues.

THE GOOD NEWS IS THAT THERE ARE OTHER FAMILY MEMBERS AND FRIENDS OF INDIVIDUALS WITH A DIAGNOSIS OF BPD WHO HAVE BEEN THROUGH ALL THAT YOU ARE FACING TODAY. THEY SURVIVED, LEARNED HOW TO THRIVE, AND SO CAN YOU.

FOR THIS WEEK

There are times in our lives when we all need some extra encouragement and resources in order to be successful.

Is now the right time for you to reach out to get some additional support? If so, today's your day to ask for that help.

1

CHECKLIST

Check all that you accomplished (or plan to accomplish) this week.

PHYSICAL CARE

Exercised 4–6 times ☐

Balanced sleep ☐

Paid attention to nutrition ☐

Ate mindfully ☐

Used alcohol in moderation ☐

Did not self-medicate ☐

EMOTIONAL CARE

Asked for help ☐

Went to individual or family therapy ☐

Made time for enjoyable activities ☐

Practiced self-compassion ☐

Engaged in pleasurable activities and hobbies ☐

Sought meaning and purpose in my life ☐

RELATIONAL CARE

Told people close to me why they were important ☐

Established or maintained healthy limits when necessary ☐

Let go of being "right" ☐

Took a nonjudgmental stance toward others ☐

Practiced empathy ☐

Spent time with people I care about ☐

SPIRITUAL CARE

Attended religious or spiritual services ☐

Spent time with others who have similar beliefs and goals ☐

Practiced mindfulness or meditated ☐

Prayed or asked others to pray for me ☐

Read or watched things that inspire me ☐

Honored my own values ☐

THIS WEEK...

I CREATED MORE HAPPINESS IN MY LIFE BY

I AM MOST THANKFUL FOR

I FOUND PEACE OF MIND IN

WHEN IS YOUR LOVED ONE READY FOR TREATMENT?

For the most part, individuals don't reach out to me for treatment or referrals until there's a crisis. Most of us (including me) take a wait-and-see approach when it comes to getting any kind of help.

We don't necessarily want to rush in when there's not a problem or when it doesn't seem like the problem is big or serious enough.

FOR THOSE INDIVIDUALS WONDERING IF NOW IS THE "RIGHT" TIME TO GET HELP, I LIKE TO POINT OUT THAT:

- If you are in emotional pain that takes away your peace of mind, you are ready for treatment.
- If you are suffering to the point where your normal daily routine (sleeping, eating, working, and studying) is significantly disturbed, you are ready for treatment.
- If you desire healthier relationships and are having a hard time figuring out what the problem is, you are ready for treatment.
- If it seems like the solution is self-sabotaging or self-harming behaviors, you are ready for treatment.
- If you are failing to meet important vocational or personal goals, you are ready for treatment.
- If you are engaging in behaviors that go against your values and create a lot of shame and guilt, you are ready for treatment.
- If you are longing to create a life worth living that is full of meaning and purpose, you are ready for treatment.
- If you cannot solve the problem on your own, you are ready for treatment.

Any kind of pain (emotional, physical, or spiritual) sends an important message telling us that we might benefit from making changes in our lives.

When we normalize treatment decisions ("We all need a little extra help now and then...") we help ourselves and those we love. When our messages are panicky or we're issuing accusations ("You're ruining our family. Get help now or I'll...") we are probably less effective.

I've found that most individuals know when they need to get help but the missing piece is the safety that comes with being vulnerable enough to accept it. Shame, guilt, or anger rarely motivate individuals with BPD to seek the help they need.

SOMETIMES WHAT PEOPLE NEED TO HEAR THE MOST IS SOMETHING LIKE:

"I love you and I know that you're in a lot of pain. Why don't we give treatment a try for six months? If it's not helpful, we'll do something else."

or

"You mean so much to me and our relationship is important. May we please try getting some extra help with this issue?"

or we may do something radical and say:

"I know that what we're doing isn't working so I'm going to get some help."

A collaborative "we" is almost always more effective than a "you" when it comes to motivating others.

WHAT HAS WORKED BEST IN YOUR FAMILY?

FOR THIS WEEK

I'd love for you to consider what has motivated your family member when it comes to get help.

What has been most helpful for them and also for you?

CHECKLIST

Check all that you accomplished (or plan to accomplish) this week.

PHYSICAL CARE

Exercised 4–6 times ☐

Balanced sleep ☐

Paid attention to nutrition ☐

Ate mindfully ☐

Used alcohol in moderation ☐

Did not self-medicate ☐

EMOTIONAL CARE

Asked for help ☐

Went to individual or family therapy ☐

Made time for enjoyable activities ☐

Practiced self-compassion ☐

Engaged in pleasurable activities and hobbies ☐

Sought meaning and purpose in my life ☐

RELATIONAL CARE

Told people close to me why they were important ☐

Established or maintained healthy limits when necessary ☐

Let go of being "right" ☐

Took a nonjudgmental stance toward others ☐

Practiced empathy ☐

Spent time with people I care about ☐

SPIRITUAL CARE

Attended religious or spiritual services ☐

Spent time with others who have similar beliefs and goals ☐

Practiced mindfulness or meditated ☐

Prayed or asked others to pray for me ☐

Read or watched things that inspire me ☐

Honored my own values ☐

THIS WEEK...

I CREATED MORE HAPPINESS IN MY LIFE BY

I AM MOST THANKFUL FOR

I FOUND PEACE OF MIND IN

VALIDATION MAY HELP

Using validation is one of the most effective ways to help someone you love re-regulate their emotions when things are at the crisis stage. In a nutshell, validation is all about communicating an understanding of your loved one's emotions, thoughts, and behaviors.

I was once working with a mom and dad whose daughter would get excited about school, sign up for college classes, and then drop out midway through the semester. This happened semester after semester.

I asked why she was dropping out and they told me that she would often become offended by the way the teacher spoke with other students in the class. Either the daughter thought that she was treated unfairly or she believed a classmate was. Her solution? Quit in protest.

After thinking for a moment, I asked the parents if their daughter had a strong sense of right and wrong. They reported that this is one of her areas where she engages in a lot of black-and-white or all-or-nothing thinking.

I asked, "Can you validate that? Is it okay for your daughter to value fairness and justice?" They said yes. Next, I challenged them to role play ways to communicate that to their daughter without telling her that it was okay to sign up for classes that her parents were paying for and then drop out when she could no longer get any kind of a refund.

Validation isn't about jumping in and solving the problem and making someone see where they are wrong. It isn't even about fixing anything at all. It's just about letting someone you love know that you understand them.

The rule of thumb? Validate first and then offer to help with problem-solving later. If your loved one gets upset by even the suggestion that there's a problem then go back to validation.

A VALIDATING CONVERSATION WITH A DAUGHTER IN HER EARLY TWENTIES MIGHT LOOK LIKE THIS:

Daughter: Dr. Smith was late for class again. He's always late and then he doesn't give us our graded tests back for weeks. We have to turn things in on time but he gets to do whatever he wants. I can't stand it much longer and everyone hates him. I'm going to drop the class.

Dad: I know it's important to you that people are on time and do what they say they're going to do.

Daughter: It is!

Dad: I don't blame you for being upset. I would be upset, too.

Daughter: People always do this. It's ridiculous.

Dad: I'd hate to see you drop the class. Don't you have a B+ average?

Daughter: Yep.

Dad: That's terrific. You know, I'm really proud of you. I know that this has been a tough semester but you're doing the work you need to do. May I ask you for a favor?

Daughter: I guess so.

Dad: Let's figure out a way to get you through the rest of the semester without dropping this class.

Will it work? Maybe.

A similar approach has been beneficial for many of the families I've worked with.

FOR THIS WEEK

Communicating understanding is part of what keeps us connected. Getting defensive or threatening rarely helps any of us to get more of what we want in life.

How are you modeling effective communication with your loved one?

CHECKLIST

Check all that you accomplished (or plan to accomplish) this week.

PHYSICAL CARE

Exercised 4–6 times ☐

Balanced sleep ☐

Paid attention to nutrition ☐

Ate mindfully ☐

Used alcohol in moderation ☐

Did not self-medicate ☐

EMOTIONAL CARE

Asked for help ☐

Went to individual or family therapy ☐

Made time for enjoyable activities ☐

Practiced self-compassion ☐

Engaged in pleasurable activities and hobbies ☐

Sought meaning and purpose in my life ☐

RELATIONAL CARE

Told people close to me why they were important ☐

Established or maintained healthy limits when necessary ☐

Let go of being "right" ☐

Took a nonjudgmental stance toward others ☐

Practiced empathy ☐

Spent time with people I care about ☐

SPIRITUAL CARE

Attended religious or spiritual services ☐

Spent time with others who have similar beliefs and goals ☐

Practiced mindfulness or meditated ☐

Prayed or asked others to pray for me ☐

Read or watched things that inspire me ☐

Honored my own values ☐

THIS WEEK...

I CREATED MORE HAPPINESS IN MY LIFE BY

I AM MOST THANKFUL FOR

I FOUND PEACE OF MIND IN

21

ALL BEHAVIOR IS CAUSED

This is great news because once we recognize that behaviors (any kind of behaviors!) are caused by one thing or another, we're in a powerful position of potentially changing the behavior.

WE SEE THIS IN OUR OWN BEHAVIORS AND WITH OTHERS IN OUR LIVES.

Several years ago, I was consulting with a family with a 16-year-old daughter. The daughter met criteria for BPD, experienced a lot of suicidal feelings, and was engaging in self-harming behaviors. Dad's primary complaint was the disrespect that his daughter showed him day after day. She was sarcastic and demanding. He (and not mom) bore the brunt of her anger in their home.

After her first day of an intensive outpatient treatment program, he wrote me to say, "Do you know what she shouted at me when I picked her up? 'Get me an iced coffee! Now!' We need to find a boarding school right away. What we're doing isn't working."

Now I'm not one hundred percent certain what caused her behavior but I wouldn't be surprised if underneath all the anger was a lot of fear about being heard and understood. Or maybe there was fear about getting better and who she'd be if she wasn't yelling at everyone all the time. Maybe treatment was stressful and she wanted to soothe herself with a favorite drink. Treatment could have also been exciting and productive and maybe she wanted to celebrate with an iced coffee but she wasn't in the habit (yet) of using phrases such as "please" or "thank you" with her dad.

It could have also been true that she had a headache and she knew that having coffee was the first step in feeling a little better physically. She wouldn't be the first person who ever acted out when they were in pain.

What I do know is that my client didn't ask his daughter why she needed coffee right at that moment. Understanding the cause of the behavior may have helped my client anticipate and manage the behavior that was so disturbing that he felt like the only possible solution was to get his daughter to move hundreds of miles away.

UNDERSTANDING THE BEHAVIOR DOESN'T MAKE EVERYTHING ALL BETTER RIGHT AWAY BUT IT GETS US MOVING IN THE RIGHT DIRECTION SO THAT WE CAN RESPOND EFFECTIVELY WITH VALIDATION, COMPASSION, AND COLLABORATIVE PROBLEM-SOLVING.

FOR THIS WEEK

Your homework this week is to recognize the causes of one or two of your most problematic behaviors. Recognizing how our own behavior is caused may help us when it comes to understanding others.

CHECKLIST

Check all that you accomplished
(or plan to accomplish) this week.

PHYSICAL CARE

Exercised 4-6 times ☐

Balanced sleep ☐

Paid attention to nutrition ☐

Ate mindfully ☐

Used alcohol in moderation ☐

Did not self-medicate ☐

EMOTIONAL CARE

Asked for help ☐

Went to individual or family therapy ☐

Made time for enjoyable activities ☐

Practiced self-compassion ☐

Engaged in pleasurable activities and hobbies ☐

Sought meaning and purpose in my life ☐

RELATIONAL CARE

Told people close to me why they were important ☐

Established or maintained healthy limits when necessary ☐

Let go of being "right" ☐

Took a nonjudgmental stance toward others ☐

Practiced empathy ☐

Spent time with people I care about ☐

SPIRITUAL CARE

Attended religious or spiritual services ☐

Spent time with others who have similar beliefs and goals ☐

Practiced mindfulness or meditated ☐

Prayed or asked others to pray for me ☐

Read or watched things that inspire me ☐

Honored my own values ☐

THIS WEEK...

I CREATED MORE HAPPINESS IN MY LIFE BY

I AM MOST THANKFUL FOR

I FOUND PEACE OF MIND IN

MONTHLY
SELF-CARE ASSESSMENT

Over the past 28 days, how often have you engaged in these specific self-care methods?

SCORING

4	**Always**
3	**Often**
2	**Sometimes**
1	**Rarely**
0	Not applicable to me at this time

PHYSICAL CARE	SCORE
Exercised 4–6 times a week	
Balanced sleep	
Paid attention to nutrition	
Ate mindfully	
Used alcohol in moderation	
Did not self-medicate	

TOTAL SCORE FOR THIS SECTION ☐

EMOTIONAL CARE	SCORE
Asked for help	
Went to individual or family therapy	
Made time for enjoyable activities	
Practiced self-compassion	
Engaged in pleasurable activities and hobbies	
Sought meaning and purpose in my life	

TOTAL SCORE FOR THIS SECTION ☐

TOTAL SCORE PER SECTION

20-24	**Excellent!** You're doing a great job of taking care of yourself in this area.
15-19	**Very good.** Identify and address any gaps in self-care.
BELOW 15	**No one is perfect.** Is this an area of growth for you?

Remember, a score of zero (not applicable) in any area may lower your section score.

RELATIONAL CARE	SCORE
Told people close to me why they were important	
Established or maintained healthy limits when necessary	
Let go of being "right"	
Took a nonjudgmental stance toward others	
Practiced empathy	
Spent time with people I care about	

TOTAL SCORE FOR THIS SECTION

SPIRITUAL CARE	SCORE
Attended religious or spiritual services	
Spent time with others who have similar beliefs and goals	
Practiced mindfulness or meditated	
Prayed or asked others to pray for me	
Read or watched things that inspire me	
Honored my own values	

TOTAL SCORE FOR THIS SECTION

9-1-1 IDEAS FOR FAMILIES IN CRISIS

Because life is messy, sometimes we need emergency skills and ideas ready to go at a moment's notice. You may already be an expert at handling emergencies but if you need additional ideas, you may want to consider the following steps.

DON'T MAKE A BAD SITUATION WORSE

Your goal as a family member or friend is to survive the crisis. One of the big guidelines we learn in DBT is "don't make a bad situation worse." When it comes to an emergency situation, we might make a bad situation worse by overreacting, shutting down, not asking for help, giving in, saying something we'll invariably regret later, judging, yelling, criticizing, eye-rolling, smacking our forehead with our hand, or by being sarcastic. Remember, sometimes family members and friends (and not the person who is emotionally dysregulated) are guilty of being the ones who may be making a bad situation much worse. That might be you.

VALIDATE FIRST, PROBLEM-SOLVE LATER

Problem-solving is rarely effective during the emergency because our emotions are just too intense or extreme. Even if we want to solve the problem, waiting until things have settled down can often be our most skillful strategy.

While it's tempting to want to make everything better as soon as possible, emergencies or crises are not the time to try and fix bigger or long-established problems.

PRACTICE OPPOSITE ACTION FOR ANGER

In order to reduce the intensity of anger, we may decide to practice a DBT skill called opposite action.

Opposite action for anger means that instead of lashing out at others, yelling, or throwing things, we make a skillful and effective decision to be gentle and kind toward the person we are angry with. This may be the most challenging skill you use in a crisis and it may also be the one that puts some immediate breaks on an emergency.

PRACTICE RADICAL ACCEPTANCE

A crisis can be a perfect time to remember that at any given moment, we only have control over what we do, what we say, what we choose to believe, and the attitudes we take toward a difficult situation.

Radical acceptance reminds us that we really have very little or absolutely no control over others. In the middle of an emergency, that may be something that helps you to stay calm and focused.

REMEMBER THAT YOU'VE SURVIVED PAST CRISES

Often it can be helpful to pause long enough to acknowledge that you and your loved one are alive and safe. If you've successfully survived past emergencies then the odds are on your side that you'll survive this one, too.

IT MIGHT BE HELPFUL TO ASK YOURSELF:

Am I choosing to be hopeful?
Do I believe in our ability to work through this?
Am I doing the best that I can right now?
Do I need extra help for me?

FOR THIS WEEK

Your homework this week is to think about what helps you the most when it comes to coping with an emergency.

What would you add to the list? What is most important from your loved one's perspective?

CHECKLIST

Check all that you accomplished (or plan to accomplish) this week.

PHYSICAL CARE

Exercised 4-6 times ☐

Balanced sleep ☐

Paid attention to nutrition ☐

Ate mindfully ☐

Used alcohol in moderation ☐

Did not self-medicate ☐

EMOTIONAL CARE

Asked for help ☐

Went to individual or family therapy ☐

Made time for enjoyable activities ☐

Practiced self-compassion ☐

Engaged in pleasurable activities and hobbies ☐

Sought meaning and purpose in my life ☐

RELATIONAL CARE

Told people close to me why they were important ☐

Established or maintained healthy limits when necessary ☐

Let go of being "right" ☐

Took a nonjudgmental stance toward others ☐

Practiced empathy ☐

Spent time with people I care about ☐

SPIRITUAL CARE

Attended religious or spiritual services ☐

Spent time with others who have similar beliefs and goals ☐

Practiced mindfulness or meditated ☐

Prayed or asked others to pray for me ☐

Read or watched things that inspire me ☐

Honored my own values ☐

THIS WEEK...

I CREATED MORE HAPPINESS IN MY LIFE BY

I AM MOST THANKFUL FOR

I FOUND PEACE OF MIND IN

RECOVERY IS MESSY

If recovery from any kind of mental health diagnosis was predictable then we could say: "She's a brand new person." or "Just a year of DBT and my depression is gone. I should have done it sooner."

OF COURSE, THE TRUTH IS ALMOST ALWAYS FAR MORE COMPLEX AND NUANCED

One day I received an email from a husband who asked if I saw much success in treating individuals with BPD. While there is no "cure" for BPD, I replied that I wouldn't be doing this work if I didn't consistently see people making progress, feeling better, and creating lives worth living.

Most of the individuals I work with for six months or longer have a significant reduction in symptoms and have a greater quality of life upon graduation from a DBT program. That's not just true for me, but it's a common experience among most therapists who specialize in treating BPD with an evidence-based treatment.

The hard part isn't necessarily starting treatment but it's staying the course when things become tough or when we begin to realize that there's no quick fix or easy answer when it comes to getting better.

It's important to have realistic expectations about treatment and I've seen again and again how any kind of progress is thwarted when individuals or their family members expect some kind of perfection in recovery.

When individuals drop out or pause treatment, progress becomes even less predictable.

The same kind of thinking is often true for most of us. I'm healthier and happier than I was fifteen years ago because I use skills from DBT in my own life. I don't just talk about them with my clients but I've made a commitment to live them.

I hope that I can say the same thing ten years from now because I intend to keep on improving, growing, and learning more while I seek new challenges in life.

YOUR FAMILY MEMBER OR LOVED ONE PROBABLY ISN'T ALL THAT DIFFERENT

I believe that one of the most important jobs for friends of individuals with BPD is to gently encourage them to not give up.

There are no perfect treatment programs and certainly I know that there are no perfect DBT therapists. If we're forever searching for the "best" then we may be missing out on some life-changing healing with what's "good enough."

Giving up too early or insisting that everything be just the way we imagine it should be sets us up for failure.

Above all else, I want for you and your family members to have more success. Perhaps today's the day to either start (or restart) a recovery journey.

FOR THIS WEEK

Your homework this week is to think about how your loved one's recovery has looked over the past six months, year, five years, or even ten years.

What kind of improvements or progress have you seen? What goals are they working towards?

CHECKLIST

Check all that you accomplished (or plan to accomplish) this week.

PHYSICAL CARE

Exercised 4–6 times ☐

Balanced sleep ☐

Paid attention to nutrition ☐

Ate mindfully ☐

Used alcohol in moderation ☐

Did not self-medicate ☐

EMOTIONAL CARE

Asked for help ☐

Went to individual or family therapy ☐

Made time for enjoyable activities ☐

Practiced self-compassion ☐

Engaged in pleasurable activities and hobbies ☐

Sought meaning and purpose in my life ☐

RELATIONAL CARE

Told people close to me why they were important ☐

Established or maintained healthy limits when necessary ☐

Let go of being "right" ☐

Took a nonjudgmental stance toward others ☐

Practiced empathy ☐

Spent time with people I care about ☐

SPIRITUAL CARE

Attended religious or spiritual services ☐

Spent time with others who have similar beliefs and goals ☐

Practiced mindfulness or meditated ☐

Prayed or asked others to pray for me ☐

Read or watched things that inspire me ☐

Honored my own values ☐

THIS WEEK...

I CREATED MORE HAPPINESS IN MY LIFE BY

I AM MOST THANKFUL FOR

I FOUND PEACE OF MIND IN

CREATING HEALTHY RELATIONSHIPS

Sometimes there's an imbalance between how much we give and take. A lot of the family members I hear from are doing their best to cope with this issue. At one point, I was working with a mom who told me, *"I give in too much."*

Since the mom didn't say, "I need to tell you about the nicest thing that I did for my daughter the other day," or "My daughter responds so positively when I'm more giving," she may have been communicating that she:

- Was having a problem balancing wants and needs for herself
- Made a decision that went against her values
- Created unwanted emotions towards herself or her daughter (like shame, judgment, or resentment)
- Put her daughter's needs before her own too many times in too short of a period

When I asked the mom for more information she said that she knows how much her daughter is hurting, and giving her things or doing favors for her helps to lessen the emotional pain for a short time.

And it's true! When people do kind things for us or give us presents, it's not only validating but it's also soothing. I certainly love it when my husband, David, completes one of my chores or surprises me with a book I mentioned that I was looking forward to reading. When we do things for each other, it leaves us feeling more connected and understood. It helps to build the relationship.

Obligational giving usually doesn't help build the relationship or leave us feeling better about ourselves. It's hard to be a cheerful giver when the giving is done under a sense of duress. I'd hate for any of us to make it a habit to give for those reasons because that's not how we want to honor the important relationships in our lives.

Another reason not to give someone with BPD all that they ask for is that invariably it increases the amount of shame they may be experiencing.

After too much giving, we may send the message, "I pity you. You can't do these things for yourself so I need to do them for you. I also don't trust that you can adequately soothe yourself so that's one more thing you need to rely on me for." What an awful disadvantage for someone who already doesn't like themselves most of the time.

If mutual respect is an issue in your relationship, it may also be true that we can often increase that respect by occasionally saying "no" or "not yet" when we're asked for too many things or too many favors. It may hurt to hear that someone won't pay for concert tickets or new clothes but it rarely destroys relationships.

Of course, you need to make a decision about what works best for your relationship. I have clients who show a lot of appreciation when they need to change a scheduled appointment at the last minute, but I have other clients who sometimes have the attitude that, "Amanda won't care if I cancel and reschedule again. It's no big deal."

THE PATTERNS IN HOW WE GIVE AND RECEIVE MATTER.

FOR THIS WEEK

When thinking about your relationship with your loved one, I'd love for you to ask yourself, "Do I also give too much or do we have a healthy level of give and take in our relationship at this time?"

7

CHECKLIST

Check all that you accomplished (or plan to accomplish) this week.

PHYSICAL CARE

Exercised 4-6 times ☐

Balanced sleep ☐

Paid attention to nutrition ☐

Ate mindfully ☐

Used alcohol in moderation ☐

Did not self-medicate ☐

EMOTIONAL CARE

Asked for help ☐

Went to individual or family therapy ☐

Made time for enjoyable activities ☐

Practiced self-compassion ☐

Engaged in pleasurable activities and hobbies ☐

Sought meaning and purpose in my life ☐

RELATIONAL CARE

Told people close to me why they were important ☐

Established or maintained healthy limits when necessary ☐

Let go of being "right" ☐

Took a nonjudgmental stance toward others ☐

Practiced empathy ☐

Spent time with people I care about ☐

SPIRITUAL CARE

Attended religious or spiritual services ☐

Spent time with others who have similar beliefs and goals ☐

Practiced mindfulness or meditated ☐

Prayed or asked others to pray for me ☐

Read or watched things that inspire me ☐

Honored my own values ☐

THIS WEEK...

I CREATED MORE HAPPINESS IN MY LIFE BY

I AM MOST THANKFUL FOR

I FOUND PEACE OF MIND IN

THREE REASONS TO OBSERVE YOUR LIMITS

There are lots of very good reasons to say "no" or "not yet" to our loved ones. The truth is that emotionally healthy people exercise their "no" muscle on a fairly regular basis. Here are three reasons why you may want to turn down requests this week.

YOU HAVE LIMITATIONS

Limitations are a fact of life. No one has unlimited resources when it comes to sharing or giving away our time, emotional energy, money, ideas, or our talents.

It's also true that there are times when we can be more flexible.

I had a client who requested that her regular appointment be moved due to an important exam she was preparing to take. Could I see her on Friday instead of Tuesday? Of course! It was something that I was happy to do since my client's academic work is important to her and I believe that it's also something that will help her to continue being successful in treatment with me.

It's also true that there are times during my day or week when I'm less flexible when it comes to moving appointments. It's not because I don't want to. I like saying yes but there are times when I cannot.

You may find that there are times in your life when you have more to give for any wide variety of circumstances and reasons.

YOU ARE FEELING BURNED OUT

Feeling burned out, annoyed by requests for help, or dreading answering your phone or seeing texts pop up may be a sign that you might benefit from saying "no" for a short period of time. It's a sign that something isn't quite right and that you might benefit from a temporary change.

This is a perfect time for you to put your own oxygen mask on first, make a renewed commitment to self-care, and to start saying no to those requests that leave you feeling physically drained, angry, frustrated, or resentful.

Now you may just need a break for a day, two days, seventy-two hours, or a few weeks. You don't have to fall into the trap of thinking that everything is either now or never or all or nothing. This is your opportunity to find some middle ground and quiet time so that you can re-prioritize what is most important to you when it comes to this relationship.

YOU ARE GIVING YOUR LOVED ONE AN OPPORTUNITY TO BE MORE RESOURCEFUL

Sometimes family members and friends are pleasantly surprised when they realize that their loved one really can solve their own problems or do things to help themselves even when they are not in a position to help.

Sometimes difficult moments resolve all on their own—without any interference from us.

If your loved one is participating in an evidence-based treatment they may be learning to soothe themselves, accept themselves and others, and also problem-solve. It's hard to do that when people in our lives are making it easy for us to do the exact opposite.

Getting our way all the time or having all of our needs met on a moment's notice means that we don't learn and build the important life skills we need to be resourceful, independent, and creative.

While people with BPD may need help, they aren't forever fragile nor always vulnerable.

FOR THIS WEEK

Your homework this week is to mindfully notice when and how you are saying "no" to your loved one. There's a beautiful, healthy balance in providing for your family member's many needs. It may take a lot of practice to figure out what is most helpful for you and for them.

CHECKLIST

Check all that you accomplished (or plan to accomplish) this week.

PHYSICAL CARE

Exercised 4–6 times ☐

Balanced sleep ☐

Paid attention to nutrition ☐

Ate mindfully ☐

Used alcohol in moderation ☐

Did not self-medicate ☐

EMOTIONAL CARE

Asked for help ☐

Went to individual or family therapy ☐

Made time for enjoyable activities ☐

Practiced self-compassion ☐

Engaged in pleasurable activities and hobbies ☐

Sought meaning and purpose in my life ☐

RELATIONAL CARE

Told people close to me why they were important ☐

Established or maintained healthy limits when necessary ☐

Let go of being "right" ☐

Took a nonjudgmental stance toward others ☐

Practiced empathy ☐

Spent time with people I care about ☐

SPIRITUAL CARE

Attended religious or spiritual services ☐

Spent time with others who have similar beliefs and goals ☐

Practiced mindfulness or meditated ☐

Prayed or asked others to pray for me ☐

Read or watched things that inspire me ☐

Honored my own values ☐

THIS WEEK...

I CREATED MORE HAPPINESS IN MY LIFE BY

I AM MOST THANKFUL FOR

I FOUND PEACE OF MIND IN

MONTHLY

SELF-CARE ASSESSMENT

Over the past 28 days, how often have you engaged in these specific self-care methods?

SCORING	
4	**Always**
3	**Often**
2	**Sometimes**
1	**Rarely**
0	Not applicable to me at this time

PHYSICAL CARE	SCORE
Exercised 4-6 times a week	
Balanced sleep	
Paid attention to nutrition	
Ate mindfully	
Used alcohol in moderation	
Did not self-medicate	

TOTAL SCORE FOR THIS SECTION

EMOTIONAL CARE	SCORE
Asked for help	
Went to individual or family therapy	
Made time for enjoyable activities	
Practiced self-compassion	
Engaged in pleasurable activities and hobbies	
Sought meaning and purpose in my life	

TOTAL SCORE FOR THIS SECTION

TOTAL SCORE PER SECTION

20-24	**Excellent!** You're doing a great job of taking care of yourself in this area.
15-19	**Very good.** Identify and address any gaps in self-care.
BELOW 15	**No one is perfect.** Is this an area of growth for you?

Remember, a score of zero (not applicable) in any area may lower your section score.

RELATIONAL CARE	SCORE
Told people close to me why they were important	
Established or maintained healthy limits when necessary	
Let go of being "right"	
Took a nonjudgmental stance toward others	
Practiced empathy	
Spent time with people I care about	

TOTAL SCORE FOR THIS SECTION

SPIRITUAL CARE	SCORE
Attended religious or spiritual services	
Spent time with others who have similar beliefs and goals	
Practiced mindfulness or meditated	
Prayed or asked others to pray for me	
Read or watched things that inspire me	
Honored my own values	

TOTAL SCORE FOR THIS SECTION

YOUR COMMITMENT TO SELF-CARE

When it comes to basic self-care, anything that helps us get through the day is a good thing. But it's also been wonderful to hear from family members who are taking the time to use the self-care section as well.

As of this writing, my first book that was written for anyone in recovery from BPD, *The Dialectical Behavior Therapy Wellness Planner* (Unhooked Books, 2015), has been in publication for several years and it makes me feel so happy when I hear from readers. In particular, the self-care checklist I originally created as an assignment in graduate school seems to be something that resonates with a lot of people.

Early on I gave a pre-published copy of the book to a mom I was working with. After using it for a few weeks she suggested that I add a few additional self-care items to the list such as showering, changing clothes, and brushing teeth. I thought, "Oh, that might be insulting. I won't include that." But, interestingly, these are items that my own therapy clients have added to their books many times.

WHEN IT COMES TO BASIC SELF-CARE, ANYTHING THAT HELPS US GET THROUGH THE DAY IS A GOOD THING.

It's also been wonderful to hear from family members who are prioritizing self-care. I have another mom I've been working with off and on for the past three years who reports that when she is not caring for herself, her relationship with her daughter suffers.

It's a great example of the transactional model in DBT: *What you do affects me;* and *What I do affects you.*

Sometimes we think that self-care is just about us but that just isn't true. When we love ourselves enough to engage in regular self-care, we also help those around us.

My best guess is that you are already engaging in a lot of self-care strategies to take care of yourself. You may also have your own ideas about what to include in a list of ideas.

What kinds of daily habits help you the most to be your best? How can you make these habits more of a priority in the weeks ahead?

REMEMBER. IT'S OKAY TO PUT ON YOUR OWN OXYGEN MASK BEFORE YOU HELP SOMEONE ELSE.

FOR THIS WEEK

What does your self-care checklist look like this week? What daily or weekly activities help you to be your healthiest and happiest?

CHECKLIST

Check all that you accomplished (or plan to accomplish) this week.

PHYSICAL CARE

Exercised 4–6 times ☐

Balanced sleep ☐

Paid attention to nutrition ☐

Ate mindfully ☐

Used alcohol in moderation ☐

Did not self-medicate ☐

EMOTIONAL CARE

Asked for help ☐

Went to individual or family therapy ☐

Made time for enjoyable activities ☐

Practiced self-compassion ☐

Engaged in pleasurable activities and hobbies ☐

Sought meaning and purpose in my life ☐

RELATIONAL CARE

Told people close to me why they were important ☐

Established or maintained healthy limits when necessary ☐

Let go of being "right" ☐

Took a nonjudgmental stance toward others ☐

Practiced empathy ☐

Spent time with people I care about ☐

SPIRITUAL CARE

Attended religious or spiritual services ☐

Spent time with others who have similar beliefs and goals ☐

Practiced mindfulness or meditated ☐

Prayed or asked others to pray for me ☐

Read or watched things that inspire me ☐

Honored my own values ☐

THIS WEEK...

I CREATED MORE HAPPINESS IN MY LIFE BY

I AM MOST THANKFUL FOR

I FOUND PEACE OF MIND IN

WEEK 10

THE THINGS WE CANNOT CONTROL

Every six months or so, we have a stray piece of mail or a package that goes to our neighbor's home two doors down and it happened again this past weekend.

One weekend I had a package that was due to be delivered on a Sunday. I looked for the package when we got back from church, couldn't find it, and forgot about it until 6 pm when there was a knock at our door. There was my neighbor with an annoyed look on her face. She said, "You need to tell the post office to stop delivering your mail to my home." She gave my husband, David, the same advice about a week before one Christmas.

And it was a great reminder of all the things we can control and those things where we have little or absolutely no control.

Honestly, there's no shortage of things I'd like to have more (or perfect) control over: David (sometimes), the cat, the temperature in my office, where the post office delivers my mail, and, of course, the future. I'd also like to have a little more influence over having my clients call me more when they engage in ineffective or harmful behaviors and it would be nice not to have to remind them about their homework or diary cards.

BUT THERE ARE A LOT OF THINGS OVER WHICH I DO EXERCISE CONTROL:

- My bedtime
- What I eat
- How I treat others
- What I wear
- How or who I validate
- How I practice self-compassion
- What I read
- How I express emotions
- My attitude when things are particularly difficult

For me, I get into lots of trouble when I start complaining and get stuck in an emotional loop when I'm not differentiating between what I have control over and what I do not. Thankfully I know that I'm not alone.

WE CAN EXERCISE OUR ACCEPTANCE MUSCLE BY:

Observing when we are fighting reality	*The car battery shouldn't die on the day I'm already late for work* **or** *They are doing that to aggravate me.*
Sticking to the facts about what happened	*David was distracted when I was talking to him and didn't understand why what I was talking about was important.*
Understanding the causes of problems when possible	*Sometimes clients forget to do their homework because they forget—not because they are trying to be difficult.*
Doing a pros and cons of embracing reality as it is	*I'll feel more at peace if I just let this go.*
Thinking about what we'd do or how we'd behave if we practice radical acceptance	*I'd be more pleasant to be around if I wasn't always so worried about the things I cannot control.*
Respecting sadness, loss, and grief that often accompanies acceptance	*It makes me so sad to think that things may never be different.*

This is a set of everyday skills that I continue to work on in my own life. Maybe you'll join me this week in working towards mastery (maybe) when it comes to helping ourselves with radical acceptance.

FOR THIS WEEK

Your homework this week is to notice those times when you are practicing acceptance and those times when it's much more challenging.

CHECKLIST

Check all that you accomplished (or plan to accomplish) this week.

PHYSICAL CARE

Exercised 4-6 times ☐

Balanced sleep ☐

Paid attention to nutrition ☐

Ate mindfully ☐

Used alcohol in moderation ☐

Did not self-medicate ☐

EMOTIONAL CARE

Asked for help ☐

Went to individual or family therapy ☐

Made time for enjoyable activities ☐

Practiced self-compassion ☐

Engaged in pleasurable activities and hobbies ☐

Sought meaning and purpose in my life ☐

RELATIONAL CARE

Told people close to me why they were important ☐

Established or maintained healthy limits when necessary ☐

Let go of being "right" ☐

Took a nonjudgmental stance toward others ☐

Practiced empathy ☐

Spent time with people I care about ☐

SPIRITUAL CARE

Attended religious or spiritual services ☐

Spent time with others who have similar beliefs and goals ☐

Practiced mindfulness or meditated ☐

Prayed or asked others to pray for me ☐

Read or watched things that inspire me ☐

Honored my own values ☐

THIS WEEK...

I CREATED MORE HAPPINESS IN MY LIFE BY

I AM MOST THANKFUL FOR

I FOUND PEACE OF MIND IN

HOW WE MAY INVALIDATE OTHERS

If you love and care about someone with a diagnosis of BPD, I already know that validation is important to you. Certainly we never set out to intentionally invalidate others. There are, however, two ways in which we invalidate others without ever meaning to.

FIRST,
WE MAY INVALIDATE OTHERS BY OVERESTIMATING THEIR ABILITIES.

When I'm sitting in front of my clients week after week and then month after month, I can usually get a pretty accurate sense of all that they are capable of. I can see their strengths and talents. I can see a particular future where they are consistently their very best. I believe in them.

But, of course, there can be a big difference between seeing and knowing someone's potential and the practical application of that potential toward an important goal. A client, for instance, may have an undergraduate degree in business but have difficulty with chronic overspending that leaves him with credit cards bills he can't pay in full each month. It may also be true that a client who can eloquently describe a particular DBT skill in our group each week is unable to use that very skill hours later after she's been in an argument with her boyfriend.

Just because your loved one can look exceptionally polished and confident three days a week doesn't mean that they can pull it off every single day. It's here where family members (and also therapists) may be tempted to assume, "He's just not trying hard enough."

But, the opposite can also be true…

SECOND,
WE MAY INVALIDATE OTHERS BY UNDERESTIMATING THEM.

If your family member has been confined to their bedroom for too long or perhaps they've been out of work or not engaged in any academic activity for a significant period of time, you might begin to believe that they can never get back to a place where they can be successful.

Perhaps they haven't given up just yet but you have. Hope feels too painful of an emotion to entertain.

I've now worked with so many clients who have the skills and emotional resilience to work five to ten hours a week with the support of a job coach or I've seen clients want to take just one class during a semester but their families actively discourage them from even trying. They remember past failures and the harm that resulted. Why try one more time?

Balancing between the extremes of overestimating your loved one's ability to help themselves and their inability to help themselves can be one of the trickiest things we do.

Not too long ago, I erred on the side of significantly underestimating a client and it's been a humbling (and really wonderful) experience to see how wrong I was. I've also been guilty of telling clients that they can "do anything" and that sometimes leaves them feeling terrified and misunderstood. Or they might imagine that they are disappointing me if they aren't able to accomplish a particular goal.

Please remember that you don't need to be a perfect spouse, child, friend, or sibling today for your loved one with BPD. Just do your best while recognizing that sometimes we all overestimate or underestimate those we care about the most.

FOR THIS WEEK

Your homework this week is to consider how you may be engaging in some all-or-nothing thinking about your loved one's abilities.

CHECKLIST

Check all that you accomplished
(or plan to accomplish) this week.

PHYSICAL CARE

Exercised 4-6 times ☐

Balanced sleep ☐

Paid attention to nutrition ☐

Ate mindfully ☐

Used alcohol in moderation ☐

Did not self-medicate ☐

EMOTIONAL CARE

Asked for help ☐

Went to individual or family therapy ☐

Made time for enjoyable activities ☐

Practiced self-compassion ☐

Engaged in pleasurable activities and hobbies ☐

Sought meaning and purpose in my life ☐

RELATIONAL CARE

Told people close to me why they were important ☐

Established or maintained healthy limits when necessary ☐

Let go of being "right" ☐

Took a nonjudgmental stance toward others ☐

Practiced empathy ☐

Spent time with people I care about ☐

SPIRITUAL CARE

Attended religious or spiritual services ☐

Spent time with others who have similar beliefs and goals ☐

Practiced mindfulness or meditated ☐

Prayed or asked others to pray for me ☐

Read or watched things that inspire me ☐

Honored my own values ☐

THIS WEEK...

I CREATED MORE HAPPINESS IN MY LIFE BY

I AM MOST THANKFUL FOR

I FOUND PEACE OF MIND IN

HOW TO STOP FIGHTING

There's an awful lot of wisdom in just letting things go and deciding that there are other things more important than controlling others, insisting on being heard, or trying to prove a point.

For the most part, many of my younger clients are open to family work or, at least, allowing me to communicate with their parents periodically.

Several years ago, I started working with a young woman who absolutely refused to allow her mother to speak to me unless it was an emergency. Even a request for a quick five minute conversation was met with great hostility.

But then things changed. My client's mother said something to the effect of, "Gosh, it's now been two years since I met Amanda during that first session. I'd really like talk to her and tell her about the progress I've seen in you." Within minutes, I received a text from my client that read, "My mom wants to talk to you. It's okay with me."

The mom and I had a positive conversation and then she told me about her success in no longer arguing with her daughter. I asked her to tell me more and she said, "I just decided that the relationship was too important so I let go of fighting with her."

Wow.

There's an awful lot of wisdom in just letting things go and deciding that there are other things more important than controlling others, insisting on being heard, or trying to prove a point.

And, if you're like me, you probably feel lousy after you've yelled or gone out of your way to tell someone what you thought knowing beyond a shadow of a doubt that it wouldn't make the situation any better. We all do it at times but it's important to recognize that yelling, arguing, and fighting is a choice that you don't have to make today. You can do something different if the relationship is meaningful.

Of course, there are other areas where we might also decide to skillfully let go or make a decision to err on the side of acceptance.

FOR INSTANCE, WE MIGHT ALSO DECIDE THAT WE'LL NO LONGER:

- Insist that someone change when they aren't ready to change
- Tell others how to live their lives
- Withhold forgiveness
- Give into hopelessness
- Imagine that life will always be challenging
- Play the role of "family historian" and continue to talk again and again about things that happened in the past.

There may be many more things that you can list. For most of us, there's plenty of room for improvement when it comes to creating healthier and happier relationships.

You aren't alone if you are struggling to find that balance between doing the best that you can at any given moment and striving to do things in a way that's much more effective.

Today can be different. While you cannot change others, you have control over your own actions and behaviors. That includes the things you do and say each day.

REMEMBER: LIFE DOESN'T HAVE TO BE PERFECT. IF YOU ARE MAKING TINY STEPS OF PROGRESS HERE AND THERE THEN THAT'S SOMETHING I'D LOVE FOR YOU TO CELEBRATE TODAY.

FOR THIS WEEK

Your homework this week is to celebrate any small successes you've made in your own life.

What's better today?

How are things easier or less challenging for you?

12

CHECKLIST

Check all that you accomplished
(or plan to accomplish) this week.

PHYSICAL CARE

Exercised 4–6 times ☐

Balanced sleep ☐

Paid attention to nutrition ☐

Ate mindfully ☐

Used alcohol in moderation ☐

Did not self-medicate ☐

EMOTIONAL CARE

Asked for help ☐

Went to individual or family therapy ☐

Made time for enjoyable activities ☐

Practiced self-compassion ☐

Engaged in pleasurable activities and hobbies ☐

Sought meaning and purpose in my life ☐

RELATIONAL CARE

Told people close to me why they were important ☐

Established or maintained healthy limits when necessary ☐

Let go of being "right" ☐

Took a nonjudgmental stance toward others ☐

Practiced empathy ☐

Spent time with people I care about ☐

SPIRITUAL CARE

Attended religious or spiritual services ☐

Spent time with others who have similar beliefs and goals ☐

Practiced mindfulness or meditated ☐

Prayed or asked others to pray for me ☐

Read or watched things that inspire me ☐

Honored my own values ☐

THIS WEEK...

I CREATED MORE HAPPINESS IN MY LIFE BY

I AM MOST THANKFUL FOR

I FOUND PEACE OF MIND IN

MONTHLY

SELF-CARE ASSESSMENT

Over the past 28 days, how often have you engaged in these specific self-care methods?

SCORING

4	**Always**
3	**Often**
2	**Sometimes**
1	**Rarely**
0	Not applicable to me at this time

PHYSICAL CARE	SCORE
Exercised 4–6 times a week	
Balanced sleep	
Paid attention to nutrition	
Ate mindfully	
Used alcohol in moderation	
Did not self-medicate	

TOTAL SCORE FOR THIS SECTION

EMOTIONAL CARE	SCORE
Asked for help	
Went to individual or family therapy	
Made time for enjoyable activities	
Practiced self-compassion	
Engaged in pleasurable activities and hobbies	
Sought meaning and purpose in my life	

TOTAL SCORE FOR THIS SECTION

TOTAL SCORE PER SECTION

20-24	**Excellent!** You're doing a great job of taking care of yourself in this area.
15-19	**Very good.** Identify and address any gaps in self-care.
BELOW 15	**No one is perfect.** Is this an area of growth for you?

Remember, a score of zero (not applicable) in any area may lower your section score.

RELATIONAL CARE	SCORE
Told people close to me why they were important	
Established or maintained healthy limits when necessary	
Let go of being "right"	
Took a nonjudgmental stance toward others	
Practiced empathy	
Spent time with people I care about	

TOTAL SCORE FOR THIS SECTION

SPIRITUAL CARE	SCORE
Attended religious or spiritual services	
Spent time with others who have similar beliefs and goals	
Practiced mindfulness or meditated	
Prayed or asked others to pray for me	
Read or watched things that inspire me	
Honored my own values	

TOTAL SCORE FOR THIS SECTION

MY POACHED EGG MOMENT

We all have our own unique preferences, histories, and experiences. Sometimes it's difficult to understand that those we care about the most have their own unique preferences, histories, and experiences that may be very different. **Why do people behave in the way that they do?**

IT WOULD BE NICE IF WE HAD THIS PERFECT UNDERSTANDING ABOUT WHY PEOPLE DO AND SAY THE THINGS THEY DO. WHEN WE DON'T UNDERSTAND, WE DO THINGS LIKE:

- Judge or condemn
- Get frustrated or angry
- Give advice about how we want others to behave
- Use sarcasm
- Engage in our own hopelessness or despair

The ability to mentalize means that we are trying to understand our own mental states and the mental states of others. A mental state might be an emotion, thought, mood, goal, belief, understanding, or value. Sometimes we have lots of evidence about what is happening with ourselves or others but sometimes we have almost none. In this case, we rely on our imagination to help us.

While mentalization is pretty different from a behavioral approach like DBT, the goal for greater overall health and happiness is the same.

HERE'S AN EXAMPLE OF MENTALIZING (OR LACK THEREOF) FROM MY OWN LIFE:

Many years ago when I was with my mother right before she died, she asked for a poached egg. I had never made a poached egg so she had to instruct me, and my first attempt at making it was a success.

Since then I've made lots of poached eggs and have grown to love them but I associate them (at least a lot of the time) with my mother.

One morning, David started to make poached eggs for us one morning and then asked me to take over so that he could get ready for work. He was prepping by boiling water in a shallow pan. My mother taught me that I needed to use a deeper, wider pan for the eggs. I decided to give it a try but the egg broke almost immediately and I quickly told David that it was his fault that the first egg broke because he was using the wrong pan.

David could have just assumed that I was in a bad mood, wanted something else for breakfast, or was upset that he asked me to take over for him but there was more to the story that he didn't know. I had a dream about my mother the previous night and woke up thinking about her. I was still thinking about her when the egg broke in a pan she wouldn't have used.

My reaction wasn't about the egg, David, or the pan. It was about a memory that is still sometimes very painful. I was able to understand what was happening fairly quickly and apologized to David for getting so upset.

If we're not personally having daily poached egg moments then we're probably surrounded by family members, friends, colleagues, clients, and neighbors who are. We just don't see what's really causing the behavior. To us, it can be inexplicable much of the time.

Understanding that we only ever see a tiny bit of what's happening with others can help us feel and be more connected to those who are important to us.

IS THERE SOME INFORMATION YOU COULD BE MISSING TODAY?

FOR THIS WEEK

Your homework this week is to identify your own poached egg moment in the past month or two. Were your behaviors easily understandable to others or was there a comprehension gap that was difficult for others?

CHECKLIST

Check all that you accomplished
(or plan to accomplish) this week.

PHYSICAL CARE

Exercised 4-6 times ☐

Balanced sleep ☐

Paid attention to nutrition ☐

Ate mindfully ☐

Used alcohol in moderation ☐

Did not self-medicate ☐

EMOTIONAL CARE

Asked for help ☐

Went to individual or family therapy ☐

Made time for enjoyable activities ☐

Practiced self-compassion ☐

Engaged in pleasurable activities and hobbies ☐

Sought meaning and purpose in my life ☐

RELATIONAL CARE

Told people close to me why they were important ☐

Established or maintained healthy limits when necessary ☐

Let go of being "right" ☐

Took a nonjudgmental stance toward others ☐

Practiced empathy ☐

Spent time with people I care about ☐

SPIRITUAL CARE

Attended religious or spiritual services ☐

Spent time with others who have similar beliefs and goals ☐

Practiced mindfulness or meditated ☐

Prayed or asked others to pray for me ☐

Read or watched things that inspire me ☐

Honored my own values ☐

THIS WEEK...

I CREATED MORE HAPPINESS IN MY LIFE BY

I AM MOST THANKFUL FOR

I FOUND PEACE OF MIND IN

25 WAYS TO VALIDATE OTHERS TODAY

Validation is the potentially powerful and life-changing act of acknowledging another person's emotions, thoughts, and experiences.

I frequently talk about validation with my DBT group members: how we can validate others, and also ourselves.

One day a group member noted that when she validated her mother, as a part of a homework assignment, she also received validation in return. My client was delighted to learn that validation helps to make room for even more validating behaviors from others.

You may be in a position where your validation of others can spark additional validation.

REMEMBER: THIS ISN'T JUST AN EXERCISE FOR YOUR FAMILY MEMBER OR FRIEND WITH BPD, VALIDATION CAN HELP IMPROVE ANY RELATIONSHIPS IN OUR LIVES.

Don't mistake validation for being nice or kind. Effective validation consistently and intentionally communicates the message:

"You matter to me.
This relationship is important."

TODAY YOU MIGHT DECIDE TO VALIDATE OTHERS BY:

1. Texting or calling a friend you haven't heard from in awhile
2. Holding a door open for a stranger
3. Smiling at someone you see in a store, bank, or post office
4. Telling someone what strengths or talents you admire in them
5. Holding someone's hand
6. Making sure someone is comfortable by offering to adjust the room temperature
7. Sending someone a thinking-about-you greeting card
8. Buying someone a small gift
9. Completing a chore for a spouse or roommate
10. Checking in on a neighbor
11. Asking someone about their day
12. Listening without giving advice
13. Anticipating an emotional need
14. Saying "thank you"
15. Asking someone for their opinion about an event, project, or plan
16. Surprising someone by making popcorn or another treat as they unwind after dinner
17. Hugging someone you care for
18. Asking, "What do you need from me?"
19. Offering to pick up extra grocery items at the store
20. Sending a care package
21. Forgiving someone
22. Texting, "I love you"
23. Letting someone know that you'll be late in meeting them
24. Encouraging someone you care about
25. Asking someone, "How can I make your day better?"

FOR THIS WEEK

Your homework this week is to notice how you are validating others.

How often are you receiving validation in return?

CHECKLIST

Check all that you accomplished (or plan to accomplish) this week.

PHYSICAL CARE

Exercised 4-6 times ☐

Balanced sleep ☐

Paid attention to nutrition ☐

Ate mindfully ☐

Used alcohol in moderation ☐

Did not self-medicate ☐

EMOTIONAL CARE

Asked for help ☐

Went to individual or family therapy ☐

Made time for enjoyable activities ☐

Practiced self-compassion ☐

Engaged in pleasurable activities and hobbies ☐

Sought meaning and purpose in my life ☐

RELATIONAL CARE

Told people close to me why they were important ☐

Established or maintained healthy limits when necessary ☐

Let go of being "right" ☐

Took a nonjudgmental stance toward others ☐

Practiced empathy ☐

Spent time with people I care about ☐

SPIRITUAL CARE

Attended religious or spiritual services ☐

Spent time with others who have similar beliefs and goals ☐

Practiced mindfulness or meditated ☐

Prayed or asked others to pray for me ☐

Read or watched things that inspire me ☐

Honored my own values ☐

THIS WEEK...

I CREATED MORE HAPPINESS IN MY LIFE BY

I AM MOST THANKFUL FOR

I FOUND PEACE OF MIND IN

OPTIONS FOR PROBLEM-SOLVING

According to Marsha Linehan, we have four options for approaching life's problems: 1. Solve the problem; 2. Feel better about the problem; 3. Tolerate the problem; and 4. Stay miserable.

1. SOLVE THE PROBLEM

While this sounds simple and traightforward, many people with BPD don't have the skills to solve their problems or they may get caught up in trying to find the one perfect or the right solution, which invariably delays any efforts to find an acceptable solution.

Long ago a friend told me his answer to feeling paralyzed by the fear of making a wrong decision: he gave himself permission to make a decision and then make another one if it turned out that the first one wasn't the best solution.

Often any attempt at taking responsibility and engaging in mindful problem-solving is a step in the right direction. We don't want to encourage anyone to wait until a small issue becomes a crisis or an emergency.

2. FEEL BETTER ABOUT THE PROBLEM

For someone with BPD, a relatively minor issue can sometimes take on a life of its own.

A flat tire or being five minutes late to a particular meeting means that they aren't worthy of good things happening in our lives or maybe it means that "bad" things will always happen to us.

Attempts at reframing the problem and seeing it from another viewpoint or the perspective of another person may be very helpful. You could also use an idea behind a distress tolerance skill by saying, "I know that today was tough but I don't think that you would have handled the argument with your boss as well as you did even six months ago. I'm proud of you for not quitting even when you had an urge to leave."

You help your loved one by gently sharing how you see a particular issue differently than they might.

3. TOLERATE THE PROBLEM

It's here where people with BPD can tell themselves, "I'm making a decision to radically accept that I'm not in a position to solve this problem right now."

Used correctly, this approach can be a great relief to someone with BPD. An example might be the dreadful period between interviewing for a job and waiting back to hear from an employer. While we can tolerate the problem, we cannot solve it in the moment. We can't force a response until the other person is ready.

If radical acceptance isn't a skill that your loved one is open to using then any of the other distress tolerance skills (such as self-soothing or distracting) may be helpful. The emphasis should be on surviving the problem without making a bad situation much worse.

4. STAY MISERABLE

If your loved one is anything like most people with BPD, they are already experts in being miserable and sharing that misery with others. It's here where you want to emphasize that any attempts at problem-solving or coping with problems are better than staying miserable.

You could also try saying or texting something like, "I believe that you can get through this." Often that's the best thing that anyone can hear.

FOR THIS WEEK

Your homework this week is to think about your loved one's approach to solving problems.

Do they assume that big problems go away all on their own?

Do they make strong attempts to skillfully tolerate their anxiety around problems that cannot be solved right away?

Or, do they need another perspective to help them see exactly what the problem really is?

CHECKLIST

Check all that you accomplished (or plan to accomplish) this week.

PHYSICAL CARE

Exercised 4–6 times ☐

Balanced sleep ☐

Paid attention to nutrition ☐

Ate mindfully ☐

Used alcohol in moderation ☐

Did not self-medicate ☐

EMOTIONAL CARE

Asked for help ☐

Went to individual or family therapy ☐

Made time for enjoyable activities ☐

Practiced self-compassion ☐

Engaged in pleasurable activities and hobbies ☐

Sought meaning and purpose in my life ☐

RELATIONAL CARE

Told people close to me why they were important ☐

Established or maintained healthy limits when necessary ☐

Let go of being "right" ☐

Took a nonjudgmental stance toward others ☐

Practiced empathy ☐

Spent time with people I care about ☐

SPIRITUAL CARE

Attended religious or spiritual services ☐

Spent time with others who have similar beliefs and goals ☐

Practiced mindfulness or meditated ☐

Prayed or asked others to pray for me ☐

Read or watched things that inspire me ☐

Honored my own values ☐

THIS WEEK...

I CREATED MORE HAPPINESS IN MY LIFE BY

I AM MOST THANKFUL FOR

I FOUND PEACE OF MIND IN

THREE WAYS TO BE MINDFUL THIS WEEK

Mindfulness expert Jon Kabat-Zinn defines mindfulness this way: *Mindfulness means paying attention in a particular way: on purpose, in the present moment, and non-judgmentally.* **That's it.**

THERE'S NOTHING ALL THAT MYSTERIOUS OR COMPLICATED ABOUT PRACTICING MINDFULNESS. IT'S JUST THAT IT'S REALLY HARD TO DO CONSISTENTLY.

Because we had a rare scheduling conflict, David wound up going to one church service and I went to another all the way in Austin one Sunday, which is an hour's drive. By the time I got back home, it was late and dark. I went to the kitchen, got some water, and began getting ready for bed.

When I woke up the next morning, David said, "Did you see that I picked up in the kitchen?" And he had! Everything was put away and organized. The problem was that I didn't notice. I wasn't mindful of what had happened. David was proud that he took charge of the kitchen but I dropped the ball in noticing.

We all do this at one time or another but it's a problem when we are missing important information on a fairly regular basis.

This week you can practice being mindful with someone you love.

1. LISTEN MORE

This is challenging. We want to talk. We want to be heard. We may get defensive (I certainly do.) We want to give advice. We want to rush in and fill the silence. One of the hardest things we do is keep our mouths shut.

This week we can practice mindful listening. We will be determined to just listen—even if it's for two or three minutes at a time.

2. NOTICE SOMETHING SMALL

When I got water from the kitchen, it would have taken just a moment to notice that everything was clean and nice. David doesn't need a lot of validation but I missed an important moment to connect with him about something that was small but meaningful.

You might notice a small sigh, change in voice tone, low pressure in the left rear tire, or a new piece of clothing. You might even notice a very small mood shift that you can acknowledge. Remember that paying attention is one of the best ways that we can help others feel validated.

3. LOOK FOR YOUR OWN JUDGMENTS

If you're telling yourself that a loved one should or shouldn't be doing something in particular, you may be stuck in a judgment. Judgments keep emotions like anger, sadness, and shame high but taking a neutral stance helps to make emotions a little more manageable.

Even asking ourselves, "Am I being judgmental?" (every once in a while) may be enough to reduce our judgments and it's an effective way to practice mindfulness.

FOR THIS WEEK

People with BPD or other mental health diagnoses don't need perfect parents, siblings, spouses, or friends. Do your best to be mindful. I think that you'll find that your new (or renewed) habits will have a positive effect on those you love the most.

16

CHECKLIST

Check all that you accomplished
(or plan to accomplish) this week.

PHYSICAL CARE

Exercised 4–6 times ☐

Balanced sleep ☐

Paid attention to nutrition ☐

Ate mindfully ☐

Used alcohol in moderation ☐

Did not self-medicate ☐

EMOTIONAL CARE

Asked for help ☐

Went to individual or family therapy ☐

Made time for enjoyable activities ☐

Practiced self-compassion ☐

Engaged in pleasurable activities and hobbies ☐

Sought meaning and purpose in my life ☐

RELATIONAL CARE

Told people close to me why they were important ☐

Established or maintained healthy limits when necessary ☐

Let go of being "right" ☐

Took a nonjudgmental stance toward others ☐

Practiced empathy ☐

Spent time with people I care about ☐

SPIRITUAL CARE

Attended religious or spiritual services ☐

Spent time with others who have similar beliefs and goals ☐

Practiced mindfulness or meditated ☐

Prayed or asked others to pray for me ☐

Read or watched things that inspire me ☐

Honored my own values ☐

THIS WEEK...

I CREATED MORE HAPPINESS IN MY LIFE BY

I AM MOST THANKFUL FOR

I FOUND PEACE OF MIND IN

MONTHLY

SELF-CARE ASSESSMENT

Over the past 28 days, how often have you engaged in these specific self-care methods?

PHYSICAL CARE	SCORE
Exercised 4–6 times a week	
Balanced sleep	
Paid attention to nutrition	
Ate mindfully	
Used alcohol in moderation	
Did not self-medicate	

TOTAL SCORE FOR THIS SECTION

EMOTIONAL CARE	SCORE
Asked for help	
Went to individual or family therapy	
Made time for enjoyable activities	
Practiced self-compassion	
Engaged in pleasurable activities and hobbies	
Sought meaning and purpose in my life	

TOTAL SCORE FOR THIS SECTION

TOTAL SCORE PER SECTION

20-24	**Excellent!** You're doing a great job of taking care of yourself in this area.
15-19	**Very good.** Identify and address any gaps in self-care.
BELOW 15	**No one is perfect.** Is this an area of growth for you?

Remember, a score of zero (not applicable) in any area may lower your section score.

RELATIONAL CARE	SCORE
Told people close to me why they were important	
Established or maintained healthy limits when necessary	
Let go of being "right"	
Took a nonjudgmental stance toward others	
Practiced empathy	
Spent time with people I care about	

TOTAL SCORE FOR THIS SECTION

SPIRITUAL CARE	SCORE
Attended religious or spiritual services	
Spent time with others who have similar beliefs and goals	
Practiced mindfulness or meditated	
Prayed or asked others to pray for me	
Read or watched things that inspire me	
Honored my own values	

TOTAL SCORE FOR THIS SECTION

ENCOURAGING NATURAL CHANGES

In her DBT skills training book, Marsha Linehan has a short section on how behaviors can be rewarded, punished, or even extinguished. On a recent Thursday evening, my DBT skills training group discussed this material. In her book, Dr. Linehan writes,

"IF A NATURAL PUNISHMENT OCCURS, DON'T UNDO IT."

Not too long ago, I told my DBT skills group that I got a speeding ticket driving through a small neighboring town and that the exceptionally dull safe driver course I took online was enough to encourage me to mindfully drive for the foreseeable future.

For most of us, these everyday experiences, encounters, and mistakes provide wonderful learning opportunities. Often they are our best learning opportunities because we're the ones who are making the connection between various behaviors and consequences.

But sometimes that learning doesn't come quite so easily for individuals with a mental health diagnosis. Maybe they lack self-awareness or perhaps they're too busy trying to survive from one crisis to the next and any kind of learning is almost always secondary. It's also true that individuals with BPD may have a lot of clarity and insight about other people's behaviors but that it's exceptionally challenging to see how our own behaviors affect or influence others.

When it comes to a family member's role in teaching, it's one thing for a parent to say, "Don't go over the speed limit. You'll get an expensive ticket;" but there's a far greater opportunity for learning when we are solely responsible for the full payment of the ticket after we are caught speeding.

The downside is that it's sometimes a painful, embarrassing, and expensive way to learn. We might even tell ourselves later, "If only I did what my parents told me to do!"

Of course, if your loved one needs help in understanding how to pay the ticket, when to pay the ticket, or how to ask for community service opportunities in lieu of payment then you should definitely help with that important aspect of problem-solving. One hundred percent of the time, I believe that's the most compassionate and effective road any family member can take. You are helping without increasing their shame, interfering, taking complete control of the situation, or removing the natural punishment for the person you love so much.

ONE OF BIG GOALS IN DBT IS TO CREATE A LIFE WORTH LIVING. NONE OF US CAN CREATE HAPPY AND FULFILLING LIVES WITHOUT LEARNING FROM OUR MISTAKES.

FOR THIS WEEK

Consider how often you are allowing your family member to make mistakes that they can learn from.

17

CHECKLIST

Check all that you accomplished (or plan to accomplish) this week.

PHYSICAL CARE

Exercised 4-6 times ☐

Balanced sleep ☐

Paid attention to nutrition ☐

Ate mindfully ☐

Used alcohol in moderation ☐

Did not self-medicate ☐

EMOTIONAL CARE

Asked for help ☐

Went to individual or family therapy ☐

Made time for enjoyable activities ☐

Practiced self-compassion ☐

Engaged in pleasurable activities and hobbies ☐

Sought meaning and purpose in my life ☐

RELATIONAL CARE

Told people close to me why they were important ☐

Established or maintained healthy limits when necessary ☐

Let go of being "right" ☐

Took a nonjudgmental stance toward others ☐

Practiced empathy ☐

Spent time with people I care about ☐

SPIRITUAL CARE

Attended religious or spiritual services ☐

Spent time with others who have similar beliefs and goals ☐

Practiced mindfulness or meditated ☐

Prayed or asked others to pray for me ☐

Read or watched things that inspire me ☐

Honored my own values ☐

THIS WEEK...

I CREATED MORE HAPPINESS IN MY LIFE BY

I AM MOST THANKFUL FOR

I FOUND PEACE OF MIND IN

WEEK 18

COMMITTING TO FINDING THE KERNEL OF TRUTH

The behaviors of individuals with BPD are often confusing or bewildering. We sometimes make a bad situation worse when we make assumptions about why people are behaving the way they are.

Usually we're better off personally and have a chance at creating healthier relationships when we can find the kernel of truth in the words and actions of others.

THEREFORE, IT MAY BE JUST A TINY BIT TRUE THAT YOUR LOVED ONE OR FAMILY MEMBER:

- Appears to be rude because they excessively use their phone at restaurants because making small talk or eye contact with others is too difficult
- Is consistently overdrawn at the bank because they are too embarrassed to ask how to budget or even understand how banking works
- Doesn't have many friends because they believe if they reach out, they'll only be rejected and feel even lonelier
- Is messy at home because they think "Why bother?" and assume that life is just too meaningless to pick clothes and other items up off the floor
- Engages in self-harming or self-destructive behavior because they feel worthless and empty
- Yells and screams because they are so desperate to be heard or understood
- Is "mean" because the world seems terrifying, exhausting, and cruel to them at every turn
- Winds up with straight Cs one semester because they assume that someone will think that they're "dumb" or "stupid" if they ask for tutoring

In an effort to find the truth we can ask ourselves questions such as, "What's really happening right now?" or "What's behind this anger/shame/embarrassment/sadness?"

Of course, understanding the behavior doesn't change the behavior but it can get us just a tiny bit closer to problem-solving when there is a problem that can be solved.

That doesn't mean that we go around apologizing for others, making excuses for their behaviors, or jumping in to solve other people's problems for them. That's certainly not the answer! It can mean, however, that understanding someone's kernel of truth means that we often have an opportunity to change our own behaviors in an effort to help others be more skillful.

It's almost impossible to be angry, frustrated, or annoyed at others for too long when we understand their emotional pain from their perspective. You don't want to be the person who always goes around being angry, frustrated, and annoyed at the people you love the most.

FOR THIS WEEK

Your homework this week is to build your empathy muscle by understanding a little bit more about why your family member or loved one behaves in the way that they do.

18

CHECKLIST

Check all that you accomplished (or plan to accomplish) this week.

PHYSICAL CARE

Exercised 4–6 times ☐

Balanced sleep ☐

Paid attention to nutrition ☐

Ate mindfully ☐

Used alcohol in moderation ☐

Did not self-medicate ☐

EMOTIONAL CARE

Asked for help ☐

Went to individual or family therapy ☐

Made time for enjoyable activities ☐

Practiced self-compassion ☐

Engaged in pleasurable activities and hobbies ☐

Sought meaning and purpose in my life ☐

RELATIONAL CARE

Told people close to me why they were important ☐

Established or maintained healthy limits when necessary ☐

Let go of being "right" ☐

Took a nonjudgmental stance toward others ☐

Practiced empathy ☐

Spent time with people I care about ☐

SPIRITUAL CARE

Attended religious or spiritual services ☐

Spent time with others who have similar beliefs and goals ☐

Practiced mindfulness or meditated ☐

Prayed or asked others to pray for me ☐

Read or watched things that inspire me ☐

Honored my own values ☐

THIS WEEK...

I CREATED MORE HAPPINESS IN MY LIFE BY

....
....
....
....
....

I AM MOST THANKFUL FOR

....
....
....
....
....

I FOUND PEACE OF MIND IN

....
....
....
....
....
....

WORRY DOESN'T HELP

Engaging in worry has never been shown to increase happiness, compassion for ourselves or others, nor does it reduce frustration.

Sometimes we think that we're doing something productive when we devote a lot of time and emotional energy to worry. Perhaps we cannot do what we want to reduce our anxiety so we spend too much time inside our heads. Worrying can often feel like problem-solving or that we are thinking through an issue but the process really is different.

THE FEATURES OF WORRY INCLUDE:

- circular thinking
- rumination
- an inability to let go

We might even start catastrophizing and imagining that the very worst will happen. We could be in big emotional trouble if we do this too often.

As a way to keep worry in check, it might be beneficial to mindfully worry for a few minutes at a time. It's here where we would say to ourselves, "For 15 minutes I'm going to mindfully worry about my spouse. I'm not going to do anything else during that time. I won't drive, do the dishes, make the bed, nor will I think about what we're having for dinner. I will only sit here quietly and worry."

This is an example of worry put in its proper place. We don't lose ourselves in worry. It doesn't consume us or our lives for very long. Once the 15 minutes is over, we move on to doing something more interesting or productive or we decide to take steps towards solving the problem that is worrying us in the first place.

Ideally, we may find that we start to worry and then quickly move on to problem-solving.

THIS REQUIRES TAKING THE TIME TO WRITE OUT IMPORTANT STEPS.

1. **Identify the problem.** It's here where you want to be as specific as possible. Don't get caught up in judgments or assumptions. Just stick to the facts and state the problem.
2. **Generate as many potential solutions as possible.** The more, the merrier! Write down all of your brilliant, silly, funny, or impossible solutions. Don't be tempted by thoughts of, "This won't work." It's here where you are using your mind to come up with lots of ideas.
3. **Identify potential solutions.** Narrow your list to two or three options that may work.
4. **List the pros and cons of each option.** Stick to the facts and be objective as possible. You could even ask yourself how the list could be seen by a neutral observer. What would they notice about your pros and cons?
5. **Decide to act.** Acting is hard but not impossible. If you find that fear is overwhelming you, go back to the mindful worry exercise above. Decide to act in spite of any fear or doubt.
6. **When necessary, go to plan B, C, or D.** Sometimes we don't get it right the first time and that's perfectly okay. Now is not the time to quit or give up. What are your next steps?

PROBLEM-SOLVING IS A SKILL THAT TAKES EXTENDED PRACTICE. PLEASE DON'T EVER THINK THAT YOU'RE POWERLESS.

FOR THIS WEEK

For your homework this week I'd love for you to challenge yourself to let go of mindless worrying in the next few days. How can you potentially improve your problem-solving skills?

19

CHECKLIST

Check all that you accomplished (or plan to accomplish) this week.

PHYSICAL CARE

Exercised 4-6 times ☐

Balanced sleep ☐

Paid attention to nutrition ☐

Ate mindfully ☐

Used alcohol in moderation ☐

Did not self-medicate ☐

EMOTIONAL CARE

Asked for help ☐

Went to individual or family therapy ☐

Made time for enjoyable activities ☐

Practiced self-compassion ☐

Engaged in pleasurable activities and hobbies ☐

Sought meaning and purpose in my life ☐

RELATIONAL CARE

Told people close to me why they were important ☐

Established or maintained healthy limits when necessary ☐

Let go of being "right" ☐

Took a nonjudgmental stance toward others ☐

Practiced empathy ☐

Spent time with people I care about ☐

SPIRITUAL CARE

Attended religious or spiritual services ☐

Spent time with others who have similar beliefs and goals ☐

Practiced mindfulness or meditated ☐

Prayed or asked others to pray for me ☐

Read or watched things that inspire me ☐

Honored my own values ☐

THIS WEEK...

I CREATED MORE HAPPINESS IN MY LIFE BY

I AM MOST THANKFUL FOR

I FOUND PEACE OF MIND IN

WEEK 20

IT'S OKAY TO SAY NO

In a healthy adult relationship we occasionally say "no" to one another. That's true when it comes to professional colleagues, clients, bosses, and it's certainly accurate when it comes to dealing with family members and friends.

It's not that others are trying to take advantage of us (although that may happen sometimes); it's that we have limited financial, emotional, and physical resources. We simply cannot be everything to everyone all the time. No one can. We all have limits at one time or another.

YOU MIGHT SAY NO WHEN:

- You need additional time to take care of yourself
- You are saving money for a bigger expense or to cover important healthcare or retirement needs
- You are physically tired or sick
- Your personal or professional goals may be jeopardized by giving in to others
- Life is already too overwhelming
- Other things demand your immediate attention
- You are practicing to say "no" more frequently so that it becomes easier
- You need time to figure out what your priorities are

For individuals with a diagnosis of BPD, being on the receiving end of giving can often increase a sense of shame and guilt. It can make your family member feel like they cannot take care of themselves when maybe the truth is that there are many ways where they are highly competent. Too much giving may actually reinforce feelings of hopelessness and helplessness.

For those times when you must say no or choose to say no, the best way for you to help your loved one might be to say, "We have faith in you to take care of this," or "I know that you can get through this day."

MAYBE SAYING "NO" OCCASIONALLY COULD ACTUALLY STRENGTHEN YOUR RELATIONSHIP.

FOR THIS WEEK

For your homework, keep track of how often you are saying yes versus saying no. What is a healthy balance in your current relationship? How are you taking care of yourself while trying to take care of others?

20

CHECKLIST

Check all that you accomplished (or plan to accomplish) this week.

PHYSICAL CARE

Exercised 4-6 times ☐

Balanced sleep ☐

Paid attention to nutrition ☐

Ate mindfully ☐

Used alcohol in moderation ☐

Did not self-medicate ☐

EMOTIONAL CARE

Asked for help ☐

Went to individual or family therapy ☐

Made time for enjoyable activities ☐

Practiced self-compassion ☐

Engaged in pleasurable activities and hobbies ☐

Sought meaning and purpose in my life ☐

RELATIONAL CARE

Told people close to me why they were important ☐

Established or maintained healthy limits when necessary ☐

Let go of being "right" ☐

Took a nonjudgmental stance toward others ☐

Practiced empathy ☐

Spent time with people I care about ☐

SPIRITUAL CARE

Attended religious or spiritual services ☐

Spent time with others who have similar beliefs and goals ☐

Practiced mindfulness or meditated ☐

Prayed or asked others to pray for me ☐

Read or watched things that inspire me ☐

Honored my own values ☐

THIS WEEK...

I CREATED MORE HAPPINESS IN MY LIFE BY

I AM MOST THANKFUL FOR

I FOUND PEACE OF MIND IN

MONTHLY

SELF-CARE ASSESSMENT

Over the past 28 days, how often have you engaged in these specific self-care methods?

PHYSICAL CARE	SCORE
Exercised 4–6 times a week	
Balanced sleep	
Paid attention to nutrition	
Ate mindfully	
Used alcohol in moderation	
Did not self-medicate	

TOTAL SCORE FOR THIS SECTION

EMOTIONAL CARE	SCORE
Asked for help	
Went to individual or family therapy	
Made time for enjoyable activities	
Practiced self-compassion	
Engaged in pleasurable activities and hobbies	
Sought meaning and purpose in my life	

TOTAL SCORE FOR THIS SECTION

TOTAL SCORE PER SECTION

20-24	**Excellent!** You're doing a great job of taking care of yourself in this area.
15-19	**Very good.** Identify and address any gaps in self-care.
BELOW 15	**No one is perfect.** Is this an area of growth for you?

Remember, a score of zero (not applicable) in any area may lower your section score.

RELATIONAL CARE	SCORE
Told people close to me why they were important	
Established or maintained healthy limits when necessary	
Let go of being "right"	
Took a nonjudgmental stance toward others	
Practiced empathy	
Spent time with people I care about	

TOTAL SCORE FOR THIS SECTION

SPIRITUAL CARE	SCORE
Attended religious or spiritual services	
Spent time with others who have similar beliefs and goals	
Practiced mindfulness or meditated	
Prayed or asked others to pray for me	
Read or watched things that inspire me	
Honored my own values	

TOTAL SCORE FOR THIS SECTION

SOMETIMES FAMILIES MAKE THINGS WORSE

One of the guidelines I strongly encourage clients to follow in DBT is the idea that we don't want to make a bad situation worse when things are beginning to fall apart.

As you already know, people who have been diagnosed with BPD have a hard time regulating their behaviors after exposure to an emotional trigger or particular events. These events can range from anything like a frown from someone they care about, a long pause in a conversation where validation is desperately sought, or when they mysteriously haven't heard back from a friend they had been texting just minutes before.

UNFORTUNATELY, SOMETIMES FAMILY MEMBERS AND FRIENDS CAN MAKE A BAD SITUATION WORSE BY DOING THINGS LIKE:

- Not understanding your own emotional vulnerabilities (such as being overly tired, sick, hungry, or needing a break after a long day at work)
- Being willful (or stubborn) instead of willing and focusing on being effective in the moment
- Interfering with the natural consequences of legal action (arrests, probation violations, no contact orders, lawsuits)
- Loaning or giving money that you cannot afford to spare (borrowing against retirement funds, securing a second mortgage, using credit cards that you cannot pay off each month)
- Tolerating physical fights
- Invalidating your own thoughts, emotions, and experiences
- Intentionally ignoring problems of self-medicating or addiction
- Not asking for help or support
- Rarely saying "no" or "not yet"
- Not attending family treatment sessions or taking part in your own therapy
- Issuing ultimatums and then backing down again and again

One day I had a mom in my office who insisted that she cannot "win" in the daily battles with her adolescent daughter no matter what she does. She admitted that she is most at peace when her daughter is out of the house and said that she didn't know how much longer she could keep up the ruse that everything was fine. She was feeling hopeless. I agreed that for right now she's absolutely correct. Everything at home has been unusually chaotic and stressful.

But when I asked her how she was taking care of herself, she said that she hadn't been doing such a great job. The exercise equipment in their home had gone unused. She was too busy with work. The mom hadn't had a massage (something she finds consistently helpful) in over a month.

One of the ideas I love most from Marsha Linehan is the dialectic (the integration of opposites) that people with BPD are doing the best that they can (and I believe that's true) and, at the same time, people with BPD must try harder to improve (I agree with this one, too).

Perhaps the same can be said of family members and friends. (It's certainly true for therapists!) You are also doing the best that you can and perhaps there's also room for some improvement in your own life.

Even though it's hard, maybe saying no every once in a while would be a good idea for everyone or you could be using more DBT skills to help yourself when it feels like you are in situations where you can't win no matter what you do or say.

FOR THIS WEEK

Your homework this week is to notice those times when you (not your loved one) may be making a bad situation worse. I know that you're doing the best that you can (you really are) but where are your areas for self-improvement?

21

CHECKLIST

Check all that you accomplished
(or plan to accomplish) this week.

PHYSICAL CARE

Exercised 4–6 times ☐

Balanced sleep ☐

Paid attention to nutrition ☐

Ate mindfully ☐

Used alcohol in moderation ☐

Did not self-medicate ☐

EMOTIONAL CARE

Asked for help ☐

Went to individual or family therapy ☐

Made time for enjoyable activities ☐

Practiced self-compassion ☐

Engaged in pleasurable activities and hobbies ☐

Sought meaning and purpose in my life ☐

RELATIONAL CARE

Told people close to me why they were important ☐

Established or maintained healthy limits when necessary ☐

Let go of being "right" ☐

Took a nonjudgmental stance toward others ☐

Practiced empathy ☐

Spent time with people I care about ☐

SPIRITUAL CARE

Attended religious or spiritual services ☐

Spent time with others who have similar beliefs and goals ☐

Practiced mindfulness or meditated ☐

Prayed or asked others to pray for me ☐

Read or watched things that inspire me ☐

Honored my own values ☐

THIS WEEK...

I CREATED MORE HAPPINESS IN MY LIFE BY

I AM MOST THANKFUL FOR

I FOUND PEACE OF MIND IN

ARE YOU UNDERMINING YOUR LOVED ONE'S RECOVERY?

Most family members do not undermine their loved one's success. They are supportive, encouraging, and do whatever it is that they need to do to help increase the likelihood of recovery.

Certainly I've never met anyone who has intentionally sabotaged a family member's efforts at recovery. However, there are some things I see family members do that can subtly derail any chance at success.

BEING INCONSISTENT

Are you guilty of making a big deal out of a behavior one week and then ignoring it the next? Do you send inconsistent messages to your family members about the important changes you want to see? Do you "give in" often?

This isn't about mindfully setting a limit and then communicating why you've changed your mind. If you are ignoring a behavior one week, punishing it the next, and then potentially rewarding it the third week then your family member is going to be very confused.

Being consistent in our expectations about another person's behaviors can also be a great way to express both self-respect and show that you can be trusted.

NOT ALLOWING A FAMILY MEMBER AN OPPORTUNITY TO EXPERIENCE THE NATURAL CONSEQUENCES OF THEIR ACTIONS

I remind all of my clients about their individual appointments the day before they are scheduled but that doesn't mean that clients still don't forget or decide at the last minute that they would rather be doing something else. I charge for cancellations with less than 24 hours' notice and have been discouraged that so many family members don't pass along my fee to their loved one.

Even if my clients cannot pay the full amount, I can imagine that being held responsible for just ten percent would send an important message about consequences.

The same goes for family members always paying for speeding/parking tickets, late fees on credit cards or for rent, or buying groceries again because that money was spent impulsively on clothes or concert tickets.

Emotionally healthy people accept (even when there's reluctance) that there are consequences to their actions. You really do want for your loved one to be an emotionally healthy person.

REFUSING TO MAKE A GENTLE PUSH TOWARDS CHANGE

Sometimes I hear, "We're just so happy there hasn't been any drama lately. If she wants to stay in her room watching Netflix then that's better than fighting and screaming."

I don't disagree with this and, yet, watching Netflix for hours on end every single day is not a part of a life worth living for anyone. Your loved one doesn't need to become an expert in reality TV. She needs the necessary life skills so that she can get up most days and engage in meaningful activity such as working, attending school, or volunteering consistently.

People with BPD don't need someone to engage in daily hand-wringing over their future but to ignore the therapeutic role of work indefinitely is not helpful.

If work isn't an issue then perhaps a gentle push may look like more greater family involvement during holidays or special occasions or taking on additional financial responsibilities.

There's a balance between acceptance and change. Gently pushing for change can be a very good thing for everyone.

FOR THIS WEEK

Do you ever undermine your loved one's success in any of these three ways?

Is there someone else in your family who might be doing this?

CHECKLIST

Check all that you accomplished
(or plan to accomplish) this week.

PHYSICAL CARE

Exercised 4–6 times ☐

Balanced sleep ☐

Paid attention to nutrition ☐

Ate mindfully ☐

Used alcohol in moderation ☐

Did not self-medicate ☐

EMOTIONAL CARE

Asked for help ☐

Went to individual or family therapy ☐

Made time for enjoyable activities ☐

Practiced self-compassion ☐

Engaged in pleasurable activities and hobbies ☐

Sought meaning and purpose in my life ☐

RELATIONAL CARE

Told people close to me why they were important ☐

Established or maintained healthy limits when necessary ☐

Let go of being "right" ☐

Took a nonjudgmental stance toward others ☐

Practiced empathy ☐

Spent time with people I care about ☐

SPIRITUAL CARE

Attended religious or spiritual services ☐

Spent time with others who have similar beliefs and goals ☐

Practiced mindfulness or meditated ☐

Prayed or asked others to pray for me ☐

Read or watched things that inspire me ☐

Honored my own values ☐

THIS WEEK...

I CREATED MORE HAPPINESS IN MY LIFE BY

I AM MOST THANKFUL FOR

I FOUND PEACE OF MIND IN

IT'S NOT PERSONAL

The behaviors of someone with a diagnosis of BPD can feel very personal but that doesn't mean that's the intent of your family member or loved one.

One day I had a mom and a teenage daughter in my office. Both were in tears and the mom asked me pleadingly, "Why does she hate me so much?" Because I like for everyone to get along (especially while they're in my office), I turned to the daughter and said, "You don't hate your mom, right?" But the daughter insisted that sometimes she did hate her mom.

I wasn't expecting her to say that but she did.

However, the session became an opportunity for the three of us to talk about how we can sometimes take out our frustrations, anger, disappointment, and shame on others but it doesn't mean that our frustrations, anger, disappointment, and shame are about anyone else but us.

It's one thing to know this in our hearts but it's another thing to remember this when someone is yelling and telling us that we're the reason why they're so miserable, depressed, and self-injurious all the time.

The same goes for work colleagues who are just about to miss a deadline, people we see in the grocery store who are worried about a family member at home, and the drivers who scream at us when we make the rare mistake of using our turn signals a little too late.

We may think that someone else's bad mood, frown, or sadness is all about us but it usually has nothing to do with anything we've said or done.

WHEN WE ARE TEMPTED TO BELIEVE THAT SOMETHING MAY BE TRUE, WE CAN HELP OURSELVES BY ASKING:

- Do I know this is true when I'm feeling calm and centered?
- What evidence do I have that this is true?
- Would someone else believe that this is true?
- Are there any other explanations or ideas to be explored before I believe this is true?
- Am I ready to accept responsibility for anything I may have said or done where I inadvertently added to another person's emotional pain?

While we don't always know what others are thinking and feeling, we can sometimes come close.

WHERE AND HOW ARE YOU DISCOVERING TRUTH IN YOUR RELATIONSHIPS?

FOR THIS WEEK

How often are you making assumptions
based on what your family member
says or does?
Are your perceptions ever incorrect?
Are you remembering that it's often
not personal?

23

CHECKLIST

Check all that you accomplished
(or plan to accomplish) this week.

PHYSICAL CARE

Exercised 4-6 times ☐

Balanced sleep ☐

Paid attention to nutrition ☐

Ate mindfully ☐

Used alcohol in moderation ☐

Did not self-medicate ☐

EMOTIONAL CARE

Asked for help ☐

Went to individual or family therapy ☐

Made time for enjoyable activities ☐

Practiced self-compassion ☐

Engaged in pleasurable activities and hobbies ☐

Sought meaning and purpose in my life ☐

RELATIONAL CARE

Told people close to me why they were important ☐

Established or maintained healthy limits when necessary ☐

Let go of being "right" ☐

Took a nonjudgmental stance toward others ☐

Practiced empathy ☐

Spent time with people I care about ☐

SPIRITUAL CARE

Attended religious or spiritual services ☐

Spent time with others who have similar beliefs and goals ☐

Practiced mindfulness or meditated ☐

Prayed or asked others to pray for me ☐

Read or watched things that inspire me ☐

Honored my own values ☐

THIS WEEK...

**I CREATED MORE
HAPPINESS IN MY LIFE BY**

**I AM MOST
THANKFUL FOR**

**I FOUND PEACE
OF MIND IN**

YOUR LIFE WORTH LIVING

A few years ago, I was working with a very kind young man whose mom quit her job to devote her days to managing her son's symptoms.

I wanted to understand more so when I asked the mom about this decision she said, "Well, he kept calling me at work and I was always running home in the middle of the day to take care of him." This sounded like a chaotic way to live and when I asked the mom if she missed her career she admitted that she had received a lot of satisfaction from her work. She especially missed the people she worked with.

THERE ARE A COUPLE OF CORE GOALS IN DBT:

- **Get to a point where you no longer need therapy.** Clients are very much encouraged to become their own therapists; and,
- **To build a life worth living.**

Unfortunately I work with lots of families where everyone is so caught up in trying to control the symptoms and behaviors of BPD that no one in the immediate family has anything that looks like a life worth living. **Do you?**

A LIFE WORTH LIVING MIGHT MEAN THAT WE:

- Are taking time for other family members and friends
- Enjoy hobbies or enjoyable activities
- Occasionally go on vacations (even short ones)
- Engage in regular physical activity
- Are working towards important and bigger goals
- Seek support and encouragement when needed
- Find ways to inspire others or allow ourselves to be inspired

This isn't about ignoring your family member's needs. I personally believe that sacrifice can be virtuous but if you are always putting yourself last then it's a problem.

The client I was working with got better. After learning the DBT skills, he was able to tolerate his own distressing emotions and thoughts, could soothe himself, and no longer needed to call his mom up to two dozen times a day. Things still aren't perfect but the daily phone calls soon just took fifteen or twenty minutes instead of hours on end.

I haven't spoken with my client's mom in months but I do know that she's started to volunteer again for a cause she's passionate about.

PLEASE DON'T PUT YOUR LIFE ON PAUSE FOREVER.

FOR THIS WEEK

What does your "life worth living" look like today? Are you taking care of your own emotional, physical, and spiritual needs or are you waiting for the person in your life with BPD to recover?

24

CHECKLIST

Check all that you accomplished (or plan to accomplish) this week.

PHYSICAL CARE

Exercised 4–6 times ☐

Balanced sleep ☐

Paid attention to nutrition ☐

Ate mindfully ☐

Used alcohol in moderation ☐

Did not self-medicate ☐

EMOTIONAL CARE

Asked for help ☐

Went to individual or family therapy ☐

Made time for enjoyable activities ☐

Practiced self-compassion ☐

Engaged in pleasurable activities and hobbies ☐

Sought meaning and purpose in my life ☐

RELATIONAL CARE

Told people close to me why they were important ☐

Established or maintained healthy limits when necessary ☐

Let go of being "right" ☐

Took a nonjudgmental stance toward others ☐

Practiced empathy ☐

Spent time with people I care about ☐

SPIRITUAL CARE

Attended religious or spiritual services ☐

Spent time with others who have similar beliefs and goals ☐

Practiced mindfulness or meditated ☐

Prayed or asked others to pray for me ☐

Read or watched things that inspire me ☐

Honored my own values ☐

THIS WEEK...

I CREATED MORE HAPPINESS IN MY LIFE BY

I AM MOST THANKFUL FOR

I FOUND PEACE OF MIND IN

MONTHLY

SELF-CARE ASSESSMENT

Over the past 28 days, how often have you engaged in these specific self-care methods?

SCORING

4	**Always**
3	**Often**
2	**Sometimes**
1	**Rarely**
0	Not applicable to me at this time

PHYSICAL CARE	SCORE
Exercised 4–6 times a week	
Balanced sleep	
Paid attention to nutrition	
Ate mindfully	
Used alcohol in moderation	
Did not self-medicate	

TOTAL SCORE FOR THIS SECTION

EMOTIONAL CARE	SCORE
Asked for help	
Went to individual or family therapy	
Made time for enjoyable activities	
Practiced self-compassion	
Engaged in pleasurable activities and hobbies	
Sought meaning and purpose in my life	

TOTAL SCORE FOR THIS SECTION

TOTAL SCORE PER SECTION

20-24	**Excellent!** You're doing a great job of taking care of yourself in this area.
15-19	**Very good.** Identify and address any gaps in self-care.
BELOW 15	**No one is perfect.** Is this an area of growth for you?

Remember, a score of zero (not applicable) in any area may lower your section score.

RELATIONAL CARE	SCORE
Told people close to me why they were important	
Established or maintained healthy limits when necessary	
Let go of being "right"	
Took a nonjudgmental stance toward others	
Practiced empathy	
Spent time with people I care about	

TOTAL SCORE FOR THIS SECTION ☐

SPIRITUAL CARE	SCORE
Attended religious or spiritual services	
Spent time with others who have similar beliefs and goals	
Practiced mindfulness or meditated	
Prayed or asked others to pray for me	
Read or watched things that inspire me	
Honored my own values	

TOTAL SCORE FOR THIS SECTION ☐

WHEN YOUR LOVED ONE DOESN'T LIKE PRAISE

While most people with BPD shy away from any kind of kudos, they are often eager for acceptance, reassurance, and recognition for their hard work when it comes to treatment and improving their lives.

One of my flaws as a therapist is giving my clients too much praise.

The truth is that I have pom poms in my office and frequently cheerlead clients just for showing up to appointments on time or completing their diary cards. I just get so excited because I know that DBT requires a lot of hard work and commitment.

Now I'm not wrong in telling them how well I think they're doing or how much I believe in them but when they start to scowl or shrink back as a result of my enthusiasm over the tiniest bit of progress, I need to honor that and stop pushing for a big smile.

Dr. Linehan considers the inability to accept praise to be a behavior that can interfere with successful treatment, and it certainly can be.

The ability to listen to kind words being said about us is an important life skill. We don't need to be perfect at it but we probably need to be able to tolerate it without self-sabotaging, hiding, or running away from any sort of compliment.

Getting better really can be very scary for most people with BPD.

Sometimes I work with parents who don't say anything at all when their child starts using DBT skills because they are afraid that they'll be dismissed (or even yelled at), but it's important to move beyond your fear and reinforce or reward the behaviors you want to see continue.

You don't ever want for your family member to think that you're ambivalent about the progress they've made.

IF VERBAL PRAISE ISN'T SOMETHING YOUR LOVED ONE CAN ACCEPT JUST YET, YOU COULD ALWAYS:

Send short little texts

"Thank you for letting me know that you were having a rough day at work. It sounds like you used a lot of skills to help yourself get through it."

"I love how you handled the argument tonight with your sister. She wouldn't stop fighting but you took care of yourself."

"I'm so appreciative that you went out to dinner with all of us. I know you didn't want to go."

"I know how hard you've been working in treatment. Let me know how I can continue to support you."

"Thank you for being so cheerful about putting all of the dishes away. It meant a lot to me."

Leave them a note or card

A note or a card can be something that's a little more personal. It's also something that your loved one can keep with them when they need a reminder to stay focused on their goals.

Consider a small gift

Small gifts can be a way to demonstrate how happy you are with their progress. Think about a gift card ($10 or $15) to a favorite restaurant or the movie theater, flowers, a book, candle, t-shirt, or other low-cost item.

Everyday consistent recognition will yield powerful results and it's also a great way to validate. Please don't think that your loved one needs big gestures to know how proud you are.

FOR THIS WEEK

If your loved one shies away from verbal praise, how else can you effectively show them just how proud you are of their progress?

What works best for your loved one?

25

CHECKLIST

Check all that you accomplished
(or plan to accomplish) this week.

PHYSICAL CARE

Exercised 4-6 times ☐

Balanced sleep ☐

Paid attention to nutrition ☐

Ate mindfully ☐

Used alcohol in moderation ☐

Did not self-medicate ☐

EMOTIONAL CARE

Asked for help ☐

Went to individual or family therapy ☐

Made time for enjoyable activities ☐

Practiced self-compassion ☐

Engaged in pleasurable activities and hobbies ☐

Sought meaning and purpose in my life ☐

RELATIONAL CARE

Told people close to me why they were important ☐

Established or maintained healthy limits when necessary ☐

Let go of being "right" ☐

Took a nonjudgmental stance toward others ☐

Practiced empathy ☐

Spent time with people I care about ☐

SPIRITUAL CARE

Attended religious or spiritual services ☐

Spent time with others who have similar beliefs and goals ☐

Practiced mindfulness or meditated ☐

Prayed or asked others to pray for me ☐

Read or watched things that inspire me ☐

Honored my own values ☐

THIS WEEK...

I CREATED MORE HAPPINESS IN MY LIFE BY

I AM MOST THANKFUL FOR

I FOUND PEACE OF MIND IN

RECOVERY IS A CHOICE

Every once in awhile, someone with BPD will say to me, "I guess I'm just not supposed to get better." Or (on a rarer occasion) I may hear from a parent, spouse, or other family member, "They just can't get better. Nothing works."

For so many people, recovery from BPD is a long journey that may take years of very hard work. People don't always have access to good treatment programs because of cost or distance. Other times, people who are wanting to make changes get discouraged and drop out of treatment prematurely or engage in self-sabotaging behaviors that derail any kind of progress

A few years ago, a friend who for many years has been in recovery from alcohol abuse told me the following story:

He was at his therapist's office talking about a habit that has plagued him for years. After going over the issue for what felt like the millionth time, his therapist let out a long sigh and said, "You know you could just make a decision to stop doing that."

He said it in such a matter-of-fact way. Then my friend thought to himself after he left her office, "He's probably right."

Even Dr. Linehan has said, "You can feel like a mental patient but you don't have to act like one." **Sometimes the truth stings a little.**

Recovery really is a choice. It can be a very brave act to face your deepest fears to get out of bed, do something new, see one more therapist, be willing to listen to something that may be unpleasant, and then not act on your emotions.

Sometimes to outsiders the choice seems simple: If you want to get better then you need to do A, B, and C. But making different choices when your head is shouting for you to hide, run, or lash out at others can terrifying.

And then there are sometimes things being reinforced in our environment that keep us stuck. There are so many reasons why people may not get better. However, I believe that everyone has the capacity to heal and recover—even if it takes a very long time.

DON'T ALLOW YOURSELF TO IMAGINE THAT LIFE CANNOT GET BETTER FOR SOMEONE YOU LOVE.

FOR THIS WEEK

Where is your family member or friend in their recovery process?

Are they working hard at improving what they can improve or are they stuck?

CHECKLIST

Check all that you accomplished
(or plan to accomplish) this week.

PHYSICAL CARE

Exercised 4–6 times ☐

Balanced sleep ☐

Paid attention to nutrition ☐

Ate mindfully ☐

Used alcohol in moderation ☐

Did not self-medicate ☐

EMOTIONAL CARE

Asked for help ☐

Went to individual or family therapy ☐

Made time for enjoyable activities ☐

Practiced self-compassion ☐

Engaged in pleasurable activities and hobbies ☐

Sought meaning and purpose in my life ☐

RELATIONAL CARE

Told people close to me why they were important ☐

Established or maintained healthy limits when necessary ☐

Let go of being "right" ☐

Took a nonjudgmental stance toward others ☐

Practiced empathy ☐

Spent time with people I care about ☐

SPIRITUAL CARE

Attended religious or spiritual services ☐

Spent time with others who have similar beliefs and goals ☐

Practiced mindfulness or meditated ☐

Prayed or asked others to pray for me ☐

Read or watched things that inspire me ☐

Honored my own values ☐

THIS WEEK...

I CREATED MORE HAPPINESS IN MY LIFE BY

I AM MOST THANKFUL FOR

I FOUND PEACE OF MIND IN

DOES A DIAGNOSIS MAKE A DIFFERENCE?

I have a general mailing list that I've now maintained since 2011. When I have people unsubscribe and give a reason, they frequently write that they were misdiagnosed and never had BPD in the first place.

This happens a dozen or so times a year. While I can imagine that this does happen, I also know that when it comes to BPD, stigma (and self-stigma) is still alive and well.

Why embrace a diagnosis that leaves us feeling so abnormal and different when we already feel abnormal and different? Isn't it easier to talk to others about our depression, anxiety, or ADHD? If there's going to be less judgment from the world, why not?

I also have clients who sometimes over-identify with the diagnosis. Even after being in treatment and having lots of success they will still refer to themselves as "borderline" or call particular behaviors "borderline" even when they have normal, everyday reactions, thoughts, and emotions. One client who made a significant and lasting change over a period of two years told me that she'd always be "borderline." I (gently) pushed back because I considered her to be in remission but was then told that was how she defined herself and her experience.

Which gets back to the question:
Is a diagnosis all that important?

As with most things, it's nice to find a dialectic or a middle path whenever possible.

Maybe it's true that a correct diagnosis is essential to a lot of people and not all that important to others.

Indeed, the extremes of complete denial and dogged over-identification will probably be concerning to most family members. We know that emotionally healthy people have a higher level of accurate and self-compassionate self-awareness. There's a difference between someone who is adverse to diagnostic labels for philosophical reasons and those who refuse to see any benefit in trying to understand what someone else may see in them that they don't necessarily see in themselves. Self-stigma ("People with BPD are manipulative, and I am, too!" or "I'm just a depressed person. That's who I am.") invariably limits people from reaching their fullest potential when it comes to getting and feeling better.

It's also fair to argue that maybe diagnoses don't matter at all. What may matter the most is steady and consistent evidence of recovery.

I'd rather have a practice full of people who are intellectually curious about why they think and feel the way they do rather than individuals who believe that they have all the answers about why they are feeling a particular way.

The latter is a much harder road for all of us to travel.

FOR THIS WEEK

Has an accurate diagnosis been important to your family member or loved one or is excellent treatment more important?

27

CHECKLIST

Check all that you accomplished (or plan to accomplish) this week.

PHYSICAL CARE

Exercised 4-6 times ☐

Balanced sleep ☐

Paid attention to nutrition ☐

Ate mindfully ☐

Used alcohol in moderation ☐

Did not self-medicate ☐

EMOTIONAL CARE

Asked for help ☐

Went to individual or family therapy ☐

Made time for enjoyable activities ☐

Practiced self-compassion ☐

Engaged in pleasurable activities and hobbies ☐

Sought meaning and purpose in my life ☐

RELATIONAL CARE

Told people close to me why they were important ☐

Established or maintained healthy limits when necessary ☐

Let go of being "right" ☐

Took a nonjudgmental stance toward others ☐

Practiced empathy ☐

Spent time with people I care about ☐

SPIRITUAL CARE

Attended religious or spiritual services ☐

Spent time with others who have similar beliefs and goals ☐

Practiced mindfulness or meditated ☐

Prayed or asked others to pray for me ☐

Read or watched things that inspire me ☐

Honored my own values ☐

THIS WEEK...

I CREATED MORE HAPPINESS IN MY LIFE BY

I AM MOST THANKFUL FOR

I FOUND PEACE OF MIND IN

FOCUSING ON WHAT'S GOING WELL

We seem to fall in love with our miseries. I know that I frequently get caught up in complaints, annoyances, frustrations, and by imagining that the worst possible outcomes are right around the corner.

Most of the time, these are little things that won't matter a month or two from now. There are little things that I grumble about that won't even matter an hour from now. They just aren't all that important.

But our grievances and moods affect others.

One Friday. I was overwhelmed with too many tasks and deadlines. I was grumpy, judgmental about my lack of productivity, and annoyed by everyone around me.

Later that evening, David and I went to one of his favorite restaurants, but because I was still caught up in my earlier frustrations, I wasn't a great dinner companion. My bad mood spilled over everything for the next several hours.

Most of the time, we have an intellectual and emotional awareness about how our behaviors, emotions, assumptions, judgments, values, and goals affect those people we love the most. But there are also times when we are utterly clueless and live in our temporary bubble of self-absorption. We have an intellectual and emotional awareness about how our behaviors, emotions, assumptions, judgments, values, and goals affect those people we love the most. But there are also times when we are utterly clueless and live in our temporary bubble of self-absorption.

If I were to make an educated guess, I could imagine that you are pretty mindful in your relationships most of the time.

THIS TYPE OF MINDFULNESS MIGHT MEAN THAT YOU RECOGNIZE HOW:

- a smile might be contagious
- your loved one feels comforted by a kind word
- asking someone about their day often prompts similar curiosity about what's new in your life
- taking on an attitude of hopefulness about your loved one's recovery may be a life-changing choice you can make again and again
- life is a bit easier for everyone when you are focused on the positive

This week you might decide to make a renewed commitment to paying attention to what is going well in life or those things that you are thankful for during your day. We might even decide to imagine that a crisis may not be right around the corner and that we can relax just a bit knowing that things unfold the way they were meant to without a lot of interference from us. Perhaps this is the week where you decide to let go of most of your complaints.

Your family member doesn't need perfect parents, siblings, spouses, or friends.

BEING THE BEST VERSION OF YOURSELF TODAY IS GOOD ENOUGH.

FOR THIS WEEK

This week I'd love for you to focus on what is going well. Even if it's something very small, what is helping you to be more positive?

28

CHECKLIST

Check all that you accomplished
(or plan to accomplish) this week.

PHYSICAL CARE

Exercised 4-6 times ☐

Balanced sleep ☐

Paid attention to nutrition ☐

Ate mindfully ☐

Used alcohol in moderation ☐

Did not self-medicate ☐

EMOTIONAL CARE

Asked for help ☐

Went to individual or family therapy ☐

Made time for enjoyable activities ☐

Practiced self-compassion ☐

Engaged in pleasurable activities and hobbies ☐

Sought meaning and purpose in my life ☐

RELATIONAL CARE

Told people close to me why they were important ☐

Established or maintained healthy limits when necessary ☐

Let go of being "right" ☐

Took a nonjudgmental stance toward others ☐

Practiced empathy ☐

Spent time with people I care about ☐

SPIRITUAL CARE

Attended religious or spiritual services ☐

Spent time with others who have similar beliefs and goals ☐

Practiced mindfulness or meditated ☐

Prayed or asked others to pray for me ☐

Read or watched things that inspire me ☐

Honored my own values ☐

THIS WEEK...

I CREATED MORE HAPPINESS IN MY LIFE BY

I AM MOST THANKFUL FOR

I FOUND PEACE OF MIND IN

MONTHLY

SELF-CARE ASSESSMENT

Over the past 28 days, how often have you engaged in these specific self-care methods?

SCORING	
4	**Always**
3	**Often**
2	**Sometimes**
1	**Rarely**
0	Not applicable to me at this time

PHYSICAL CARE	SCORE
Exercised 4-6 times a week	
Balanced sleep	
Paid attention to nutrition	
Ate mindfully	
Used alcohol in moderation	
Did not self-medicate	

TOTAL SCORE FOR THIS SECTION

EMOTIONAL CARE	SCORE
Asked for help	
Went to individual or family therapy	
Made time for enjoyable activities	
Practiced self-compassion	
Engaged in pleasurable activities and hobbies	
Sought meaning and purpose in my life	

TOTAL SCORE FOR THIS SECTION

TOTAL SCORE PER SECTION

20-24   **Excellent!** You're doing a great job of taking care of yourself in this area.

15-19   **Very good.** Identify and address any gaps in self-care.

BELOW 15   **No one is perfect.** Is this an area of growth for you?

Remember, a score of zero (not applicable) in any area may lower your section score.

RELATIONAL CARE	SCORE
Told people close to me why they were important	
Established or maintained healthy limits when necessary	
Let go of being "right"	
Took a nonjudgmental stance toward others	
Practiced empathy	
Spent time with people I care about	

TOTAL SCORE FOR THIS SECTION ☐

SPIRITUAL CARE	SCORE
Attended religious or spiritual services	
Spent time with others who have similar beliefs and goals	
Practiced mindfulness or meditated	
Prayed or asked others to pray for me	
Read or watched things that inspire me	
Honored my own values	

TOTAL SCORE FOR THIS SECTION ☐

STOP DIGGING

One of the core guidelines in DBT is "don't make a bad situation worse" or, to put it another way, "when you're in a hole, stop digging." **All of us, at times, are guilty of inadvertently making things worse.**

In my personal life, I tend to procrastinate. I'm not proactive with a lot of problems. Allowing procrastination to occur is one of the ways I know I make a bad situation worse.

Life is just more complicated. I know how to get out of my comfort zone of doing things differently but doing it is challenging, so I often need to ask for a lot of help from people in my life.

Using drugs or alcohol, giving in to despair, telling others how they should feel, or shouting over others may be some fairly obvious ways in which we can make a bad situation worse, but **family members or friends might also be engaging in other behaviors** that make life more complicated for everyone.

BLAMING AND JUDGING

In DBT, Marsha Linehan encourages us to look for the causes of behaviors rather than resort to blaming or judging, but the truth is that blaming and judging is often far easier. It even feels temporarily satisfying to judge, blame, or talk about the problem behavior with everyone else in our life instead of the person we need to talk to. I've definitely done this.

DISCOURAGING NATURAL CONSEQUENCES

Are you interfering with life's natural consequences? Do you pay for missed therapy appointments or traffic fines? Or tuition for dropped classes? Do you ever apologize for your loved one's behavior when it would be more appropriate for them to take responsibility for their actions?

Often we want to shield people we love from the difficult (and sometimes fear-provoking) consequences of the real world—even when that's not necessarily best for them.

IGNORING PROBLEMS

Sometimes we imagine that things will magically get better all on their own and without a lot of hard work. While that may happen, we want to be honest with ourselves and others about important issues that consistently get in the way of having healthier relationships.

Maybe you make a bad situation worse by putting off a difficult conversation you know should probably happen sooner rather than later.

FOR THIS WEEK

This week I'd love for you to think about how you may be making a bad situation worse.

Is there something that you may be doing that's getting in the way of your loved one's life worth living?

29

CHECKLIST

Check all that you accomplished (or plan to accomplish) this week.

PHYSICAL CARE

Exercised 4-6 times ☐

Balanced sleep ☐

Paid attention to nutrition ☐

Ate mindfully ☐

Used alcohol in moderation ☐

Did not self-medicate ☐

EMOTIONAL CARE

Asked for help ☐

Went to individual or family therapy ☐

Made time for enjoyable activities ☐

Practiced self-compassion ☐

Engaged in pleasurable activities and hobbies ☐

Sought meaning and purpose in my life ☐

RELATIONAL CARE

Told people close to me why they were important ☐

Established or maintained healthy limits when necessary ☐

Let go of being "right" ☐

Took a nonjudgmental stance toward others ☐

Practiced empathy ☐

Spent time with people I care about ☐

SPIRITUAL CARE

Attended religious or spiritual services ☐

Spent time with others who have similar beliefs and goals ☐

Practiced mindfulness or meditated ☐

Prayed or asked others to pray for me ☐

Read or watched things that inspire me ☐

Honored my own values ☐

THIS WEEK...

I CREATED MORE HAPPINESS IN MY LIFE BY

I AM MOST THANKFUL FOR

I FOUND PEACE OF MIND IN

SHOULD YOU CHANGE THE WAY YOU COMMUNICATE?

Several years ago the parent of a new client challenged me when it came to learning a few ways to validate her 16-year-old daughter. "Why should I change the way I communicate? The world doesn't work that way. The world doesn't care if my daughter feels validated."

And this mom is absolutely correct. For emotionally sensitive people, the world is pretty invalidating. People at the grocery store, at school, or at our offices are not (or rarely) asking themselves, "How can I make sure the person in front of me feels understood?" Even close friends or other people who love us may not be interested in learning a different way of communicating. For people with a diagnosis of BPD or in recovery from BPD, we'll be reminded of this fact again and again throughout our lives.

Spoken validation (and engaging in validating acts) is hard work, takes practice, and it's not always as effective as we'd like. There are lots of excellent reasons not to validate.

It's also true that my client would benefit from learning how to validate herself. Instead of relying on her mom, dad, and boyfriend for that external evidence that she's someone who's worthy and understandable, she can help herself by engaging in self-validating language and behaviors. For most of my clients, this is a pretty advanced skill and not something that is mastered early in treatment.

Also, we could make an argument that maybe we don't need others to validate us or that we shouldn't expect it. Perhaps life might be easier if we met all of our own emotional needs.

Maybe it's accurate that validation strategies could help this mother improve her relationship with her daughter. We started out our session with a lot of justified defensiveness (and this mom's anger did make sense) but when I asked this mom to tell me what her daughter was like when she was at her best, she began to soften. She told me that her daughter was compassionate with others.

She helped around the house. She didn't say hurtful things to her younger siblings. She wasn't imagining that suicidal thinking and planning was the answer to life's problems.

It was true! This described my client when she was at her best. We saw the same inherent strengths. We were on the same side.

That, of course was the reason why this mom wanted to communicate in a different way. Validation would (hopefully) increase the likelihood that she could help her daughter to be a little more compassionate, more helpful around the house, kinder to her brothers and sisters, and a little less depressed.

There's no magic formula, but that's often how it works. People who feel consistently validated are probably going to be a little less angry, feel more secure, and be more trusting of others. People who feel understood usually don't go around yelling, screaming, self-sabotaging, and mistrusting everyone they come in contact with. When we feel understood, we take care of ourselves, too.

It's one thing for the therapist to be validating an hour or two each week but think about how much more powerful, motivating, and healing it is when a parent, spouse, or best friend uses validation to help their loved one to be their very best.

You have that power today. You can use that power in the next five minutes or the next day or two. You can make a profound difference in how your family member helps themselves.

FOR THIS WEEK

This week I'd love for you to remember how much positive power you have in your relationship.

30

CHECKLIST

Check all that you accomplished
(or plan to accomplish) this week.

PHYSICAL CARE

Exercised 4-6 times ☐

Balanced sleep ☐

Paid attention to nutrition ☐

Ate mindfully ☐

Used alcohol in moderation ☐

Did not self-medicate ☐

EMOTIONAL CARE

Asked for help ☐

Went to individual or family therapy ☐

Made time for enjoyable activities ☐

Practiced self-compassion ☐

Engaged in pleasurable activities and hobbies ☐

Sought meaning and purpose in my life ☐

RELATIONAL CARE

Told people close to me why they were important ☐

Established or maintained healthy limits when necessary ☐

Let go of being "right" ☐

Took a nonjudgmental stance toward others ☐

Practiced empathy ☐

Spent time with people I care about ☐

SPIRITUAL CARE

Attended religious or spiritual services ☐

Spent time with others who have similar beliefs and goals ☐

Practiced mindfulness or meditated ☐

Prayed or asked others to pray for me ☐

Read or watched things that inspire me ☐

Honored my own values ☐

THIS WEEK...

I CREATED MORE HAPPINESS IN MY LIFE BY

I AM MOST THANKFUL FOR

I FOUND PEACE OF MIND IN

FOCUS ON REWARDS

Instead of punishing people we care about when they do things we don't like or approve of, we could always try rewarding the behaviors we want to see more of. Punishment can be subtle. Sometimes we send messages of disapproval about how others are behaving by making frowny faces, stonewalling, or leaving a room.

Punishment can also be loud. We might scream, throw tantrums, threaten others, or we might take things away (like phone privileges for a teen or we might withhold affection for a spouse).

Now punishment can sometimes motivate behavioral changes but it doesn't often work for people with a diagnosis of BPD. While I believe that punishment may be occasionally effective when it comes to getting other people to change their behavior, other approaches may be much more helpful.

But often we're too quick to jump to punishing behaviors. I once had a therapy client tell me that he had strong urges to hurt or punish others because he's been hurt in the past. He said, "I know it's wrong but I want others to hurt so they know how it feels."

Although that strategy may help my client manage his emotions for a short amount of time, it's not going to help him get along better with his girlfriend and work colleagues. Punishing others won't help him to build friendships. It doesn't make him trustworthy nor does it help him to trust others. Being on the receiving end of punishment, again and again, may be the one thing that destroys trust for individuals who are emotionally-sensitive and already believe that the world is a difficult and unsafe place to live.

For individuals with a diagnosis of BPD or another mental health diagnosis, punishment doesn't necessarily lead to significant moments of learning and permanently changed behavior.

For that reason, I rarely encourage it when I'm working with families.

Instead, it's almost always more helpful to think about how rewards or desired consequences can help to motivate more of the behaviors we want to see. In my practice, clients (especially when treatment is new) get rewarded for coming to appointments, completing their diary card, and doing their homework. I use pom poms or scented banana stickers and make a really big deal out of something small that I know is difficult. If I have time in between sessions and I'm getting myself an iced coffee, I'll text my clients who are coming in and ask them if I can pick up a coffee or juice for them, too.

I can't tell you that this approach consistently works to keep people in treatment (I definitely have people who leave prematurely) but I hope that it makes a difference for some.

You can also be that same motivating person. While you may not have hundreds of banana stickers in a drawer waiting to be given out, I know that you have something special (and probably a lot more meaningful) that you can do or say when you see your family member or loved one doing their best and trying hard.

Maybe this is your week to send or leave them a little note, or perhaps it's more appropriate to make a much bigger gesture. Frequent reminders that communicate "you're important, and I care about you" after small changes in behavior will make a difference over an extended period.

Please don't expect that you can use a reward once and the behavior will be forever changed. More than anything else, being patient and consistent will likely yield the best results.

FOR THIS WEEK

This week I'd love for you to think about what effective rewards look like in your loved one's life.

What helps to motivate them to be their very best and healthiest self?

CHECKLIST

Check all that you accomplished (or plan to accomplish) this week.

PHYSICAL CARE

Exercised 4–6 times ☐

Balanced sleep ☐

Paid attention to nutrition ☐

Ate mindfully ☐

Used alcohol in moderation ☐

Did not self-medicate ☐

EMOTIONAL CARE

Asked for help ☐

Went to individual or family therapy ☐

Made time for enjoyable activities ☐

Practiced self-compassion ☐

Engaged in pleasurable activities and hobbies ☐

Sought meaning and purpose in my life ☐

RELATIONAL CARE

Told people close to me why they were important ☐

Established or maintained healthy limits when necessary ☐

Let go of being "right" ☐

Took a nonjudgmental stance toward others ☐

Practiced empathy ☐

Spent time with people I care about ☐

SPIRITUAL CARE

Attended religious or spiritual services ☐

Spent time with others who have similar beliefs and goals ☐

Practiced mindfulness or meditated ☐

Prayed or asked others to pray for me ☐

Read or watched things that inspire me ☐

Honored my own values ☐

THIS WEEK...

I CREATED MORE HAPPINESS IN MY LIFE BY

I AM MOST THANKFUL FOR

I FOUND PEACE OF MIND IN

WISDOM FROM A CLIENT

A long time ago I was working with a client who had been busy making bad situations much worse. We spend our session talking about the skills she could have used and planning for the coming weekend.

Because her very bad days were often spent saying mean things to her husband and telling him that he didn't love her (in spite of evidence to the contrary), we also came up with a coping ahead plan with practical ideas she could use to help herself and strengthen her relationship. What could she do or say to stay on track with using her skills?

In a beautiful moment, she told me, "If I'm patient and compassionate with myself and my husband, we'll be okay."

She even wrote "patient" and "compassionate" in her notebook for her to remember.

Of course, she's right. I think that all of our relationships can be better when we are both patient and simultaneously compassionate. It's true for me, and it's true for every client I can think of.

The same advice might also be true for you.

I know that you are already a compassionate person. You, dear reader, wouldn't have purchased this book if you didn't love someone who was suffering from a lot of emotional intensity but if you are like most people, the challenge of being patient may bring you some of the greatest obstacles.

For me, being impatient often looks like a lack of faith. Instead of choosing to be hopeful and believe that things will get slowly better over time, I get nervous and worry. I imagine that nothing will ever change. I start to think that whatever is happening at the moment is going to become bigger and scarier by the second.

Any bit of patience goes right out the window when I begin to think about how everything must be falling apart.

But most of the time that doesn't happen for my clients or me.

The good outweighs the bad over and over again. On a day when I don't feel compassionate or patient, I can give myself an opportunity to remember my clients who have graduated from college or those clients who no longer harm themselves. I can remember clients who decide to practice self-love instead of self-hatred, clients who have better relationships with their families, and a client who is getting married in a couple of months.

While I don't have any perfect client stories, I have clients who are brave enough to choose compassion and patience on a pretty regular basis consistently. These clients are my personal heroes. These are the clients who go on to create lives worth living for themselves.

Today I'd love for you to do something similar. Because you cannot control others, why not embrace the freedom of choosing the attitude you'll take when, like me, you want to allow yourself to imagine that life will always be complicated, chaotic, and dramatic?

This week I'm choosing to be compassionate and patient instead of fearful. **I'd love for you to join me.**

FOR THIS WEEK

This week I'd love for you to be as wise as my client.

How often are you helping yourself and those you love by choosing to remain hopeful instead of giving into despair?

CHECKLIST

Check all that you accomplished (or plan to accomplish) this week.

PHYSICAL CARE

Exercised 4-6 times ☐

Balanced sleep ☐

Paid attention to nutrition ☐

Ate mindfully ☐

Used alcohol in moderation ☐

Did not self-medicate ☐

EMOTIONAL CARE

Asked for help ☐

Went to individual or family therapy ☐

Made time for enjoyable activities ☐

Practiced self-compassion ☐

Engaged in pleasurable activities and hobbies ☐

Sought meaning and purpose in my life ☐

RELATIONAL CARE

Told people close to me why they were important ☐

Established or maintained healthy limits when necessary ☐

Let go of being "right" ☐

Took a nonjudgmental stance toward others ☐

Practiced empathy ☐

Spent time with people I care about ☐

SPIRITUAL CARE

Attended religious or spiritual services ☐

Spent time with others who have similar beliefs and goals ☐

Practiced mindfulness or meditated ☐

Prayed or asked others to pray for me ☐

Read or watched things that inspire me ☐

Honored my own values ☐

THIS WEEK...

I CREATED MORE HAPPINESS IN MY LIFE BY

I AM MOST THANKFUL FOR

I FOUND PEACE OF MIND IN

MONTHLY

SELF-CARE ASSESSMENT

Over the past 28 days, how often have you engaged in these specific self-care methods?

PHYSICAL CARE	SCORE
Exercised 4–6 times a week	
Balanced sleep	
Paid attention to nutrition	
Ate mindfully	
Used alcohol in moderation	
Did not self-medicate	

TOTAL SCORE FOR THIS SECTION

EMOTIONAL CARE	SCORE
Asked for help	
Went to individual or family therapy	
Made time for enjoyable activities	
Practiced self-compassion	
Engaged in pleasurable activities and hobbies	
Sought meaning and purpose in my life	

TOTAL SCORE FOR THIS SECTION

TOTAL SCORE PER SECTION

20-24	**Excellent!** You're doing a great job of taking care of yourself in this area.
15-19	**Very good.** Identify and address any gaps in self-care.
BELOW 15	**No one is perfect.** Is this an area of growth for you?

Remember, a score of zero (not applicable) in any area may lower your section score.

RELATIONAL CARE	SCORE
Told people close to me why they were important	
Established or maintained healthy limits when necessary	
Let go of being "right"	
Took a nonjudgmental stance toward others	
Practiced empathy	
Spent time with people I care about	

TOTAL SCORE FOR THIS SECTION

SPIRITUAL CARE	SCORE
Attended religious or spiritual services	
Spent time with others who have similar beliefs and goals	
Practiced mindfulness or meditated	
Prayed or asked others to pray for me	
Read or watched things that inspire me	
Honored my own values	

TOTAL SCORE FOR THIS SECTION

FINDING MEANING IN PAIN

Individuals with a diagnosis of BPD often feel empty, or that life is meaningless. That meaninglessness often leads to suicidal thinking, planning, and suicide attempts. But I also believe that we can have a life worth living even when we are thinking about suicide.

In fact, making a difficult decision to live when we are feeling suicidal is the ultimate exercise in affirming our inherent value, self-worth, and determination that struggling is often a normal part of the human condition. We only have to point to the daily news to see that suffering is extraordinarily common.

Viktor Frankl was a physician and a Holocaust survivor who developed an existential treatment called Logotherapy.

THE PRIMARY TENETS OF LOGOTHERAPY ARE:

- Life has meaning under all circumstances, even the most miserable ones.
- Our main motivation for living is our will to find meaning in life.
- We have the freedom to find meaning in what we do and what we experience, or at least in the stance we take when faced with a situation of unchangeable suffering.

Individuals with BPD can decide that life is worth living and can be meaningful—even when we face the possibility of "unchangeable suffering." But a diagnosis like BPD doesn't mean a life sentence of painful emotions.

What we do know is that individuals who are acutely suicidal can take steps to alleviate their emotional pain. Five minutes of meaning-making here and ten minutes of a tiny bit of contentment there can take us from a place of hopelessness to one where life isn't quite so painful all the time.

Emotional pain may come and go, but it doesn't need to last for hours (or days) on end. We can find those little moments where the world is just as it is and we're (fairly) content.

While no treatment or treatment approach is perfect, a focus on helping people to recognize and create meaning in their lives may make a difference in how successful we are in recovery. Maybe a little extra meaning may help all of us to handle life's little (and very big) bumps a bit more smoothly.

FOR THIS WEEK

This week I'd love for you to think about what makes life meaningful to you or for those individuals you love. Instead of focusing on the pain, maybe today we can make a different decision.

CHECKLIST

Check all that you accomplished
(or plan to accomplish) this week.

PHYSICAL CARE

Exercised 4–6 times ☐

Balanced sleep ☐

Paid attention to nutrition ☐

Ate mindfully ☐

Used alcohol in moderation ☐

Did not self-medicate ☐

EMOTIONAL CARE

Asked for help ☐

Went to individual or family therapy ☐

Made time for enjoyable activities ☐

Practiced self-compassion ☐

Engaged in pleasurable activities and hobbies ☐

Sought meaning and purpose in my life ☐

RELATIONAL CARE

Told people close to me why they were important ☐

Established or maintained healthy limits when necessary ☐

Let go of being "right" ☐

Took a nonjudgmental stance toward others ☐

Practiced empathy ☐

Spent time with people I care about ☐

SPIRITUAL CARE

Attended religious or spiritual services ☐

Spent time with others who have similar beliefs and goals ☐

Practiced mindfulness or meditated ☐

Prayed or asked others to pray for me ☐

Read or watched things that inspire me ☐

Honored my own values ☐

THIS WEEK...

I CREATED MORE HAPPINESS IN MY LIFE BY

I AM MOST THANKFUL FOR

I FOUND PEACE OF MIND IN

SHOULD YOU SOOTHE PEOPLE WITH BPD?

An important part of emotional health is the ability to soothe ourselves in a way where we don't harm others, harm ourselves, or make a bad situation worse by ignoring responsibilities or by finding a way to check out of life temporarily.

Sometimes I have clients who soothe themselves by drinking, self-medicating, playing video games for hours, or they might decide to binge watch tv shows or movies all day long. While this may be temporarily effective (and maybe a better alternative to some other behaviors that may land people in the hospital or jail) is not effective self-soothing. It's not a part of creating a life worth living.

A treatment like DBT gives us over a dozen potential ways to soothe ourselves, but it can take a lot of practice. People with BPD may decide that it's not worth it to practice the ideas (the pros don't outweigh the cons) or people in their lives may be reinforcing coping strategies that are not helpful. Effective soothing (and self-soothing) is almost always an active choice rather than a passive, mindless, or self-indulgent activity.

One of the things that I like to emphasize is that we don't want to self-soothe when we can focus on solving the problem that is causing the distress in the first place. It may be obvious enough for you to imagine that if having too little money is causing a lot of anxiety for someone, the answer isn't opening another credit line and creating more debt. However, for someone with BPD, they may not necessarily see the connection. Shopping relieves the anxiety for a very short time but creates a bigger, long-term problem.

Of course, there are pros and cons to soothing others or helping people to soothe themselves.

The pros might include that happy feeling when we help others. It makes me feel glad to help others, and it makes me even happier when I can show others how to help themselves by using DBT skills in the way where my clients aren't avoiding relationships or adult responsibilities. Often people with BPD need others to demonstrate soothing activities. Family members and friends can make a difference by saying "It's been a rough day and I don't want to argue any longer. Let's go and soothe ourselves by going to the lake and taking a walk." or "Why don't we play cards tonight? It might relax both of us." Soothing others can also be an act of validation and love.

But there can be cons to soothing others. Family members might also be tempted to soothe rather than problem solve (especially when facing the problem is extra challenging), or they might want to soothe as a way of protecting their loved one from normal emotional pain. Sometimes when we try to soothe others, we wind up giving people the impression that they are too fragile or sensitive. Instead of imagining that they can successfully soothe themselves, we want to take on the burden and engage in behaviors that may look more like placating or even rescuing.

At any given moment, you might be making a difficult decision and weighing the pros and cons of soothing others or helping others to soothe themselves. **What will help your loved one the most today?**

FOR THIS WEEK

This week I'd love for you to focus on what effective soothing looks like for you and your family member.

What is most beneficial to you both?

34

CHECKLIST

Check all that you accomplished (or plan to accomplish) this week.

PHYSICAL CARE

Exercised 4-6 times ☐

Balanced sleep ☐

Paid attention to nutrition ☐

Ate mindfully ☐

Used alcohol in moderation ☐

Did not self-medicate ☐

EMOTIONAL CARE

Asked for help ☐

Went to individual or family therapy ☐

Made time for enjoyable activities ☐

Practiced self-compassion ☐

Engaged in pleasurable activities and hobbies ☐

Sought meaning and purpose in my life ☐

RELATIONAL CARE

Told people close to me why they were important ☐

Established or maintained healthy limits when necessary ☐

Let go of being "right" ☐

Took a nonjudgmental stance toward others ☐

Practiced empathy ☐

Spent time with people I care about ☐

SPIRITUAL CARE

Attended religious or spiritual services ☐

Spent time with others who have similar beliefs and goals ☐

Practiced mindfulness or meditated ☐

Prayed or asked others to pray for me ☐

Read or watched things that inspire me ☐

Honored my own values ☐

THIS WEEK...

I CREATED MORE HAPPINESS IN MY LIFE BY

I AM MOST THANKFUL FOR

I FOUND PEACE OF MIND IN

WHEN PEOPLE DON'T GET BETTER

I always do my best to err on the side of hopefulness. Over the years, I've seen far more success stories than failures. With or without treatment, most people with BPD will inch towards recovery, or they will stabilize given enough time and patience.

There may still be lots of ups and downs, but the bumps are smaller, less frequent, and probably a bit more predictable for everyone. Coping with everyday life events becomes easier although it may never be easy.

But there are instances where life does not become better or easier. Either an individual's behavior remains disruptive, abusive, or self-destructive for years or life potentially ends in suicide or incarceration.

When I'm assessing new clients, I'll look for issues, problems, and patterns that may make recovery more challenging. These include:

OTHER PERSONALITY DISORDERS

Although I primarily treat individuals with BPD, I also see co-occurring personality disorders such as narcissistic personality disorder, antisocial personality disorder, schizotypal personality disorder, avoidant personality disorder, and dependent personality disorder in persons seeking treatment. While there are clear recovery pathways with BPD, this isn't necessarily the case with additional diagnoses.

CURRENT DRUG AND ALCOHOL USE

Beyond a shadow of a doubt, ongoing use of alcohol and drugs make successful treatment more difficult to attain. A willingness to work towards reducing substance use is a step in the right direction when complete sobriety is not yet feasible.

A LACK OF SELF-AWARENESS

Many of my clients can easily connect why they are thinking, feeling, and behaving in the way that they do. For others, connecting those dots doesn't necessarily happen in the way we'd like.

Individuals who get easily stuck in seeing themselves as victims or blaming others for their problems will have a more challenging time in treatment. Thankfully, developing greater self-awareness is a skill that can be learned and cultivated over time. Evidence-based therapies such as DBT and Mentalization-Based Treatment will be helpful.

HOPELESSNESS

When I'm assessing clients, I'm not simply looking for how motivated they might be, but I'm usually more concerned with how hopeful clients are. For clients who believe that change and growth are possible, success can be easy to predict, but for those who don't think that life can become better through the hard work recovery takes, treatment outcomes may be less predictable.

A LACK OF FAMILY SUPPORT

When families are all working together towards change, I consistently feel encouraged and hopeful. But when I hear from family members that their loved one is the "problem" and that everything will be fine when they are better, it's easy for me to be discouraged. It's hard to face a mental health diagnosis when you don't have people on your side. BPD really is a family issue. Family support and education make a consistent difference. Saying (or texting), "We care about you. Let us know how we can help." is a great first step.

Understanding what may block recovery is an excellent first step towards healing. While we can't change others, we can help ourselves to cope in more effective ways.

FOR THIS WEEK

Can you identify another roadblock to recovery in your family member's life?

What is preventing them from having a better chance at recovery?

CHECKLIST

Check all that you accomplished (or plan to accomplish) this week.

PHYSICAL CARE

Exercised 4–6 times ☐

Balanced sleep ☐

Paid attention to nutrition ☐

Ate mindfully ☐

Used alcohol in moderation ☐

Did not self-medicate ☐

EMOTIONAL CARE

Asked for help ☐

Went to individual or family therapy ☐

Made time for enjoyable activities ☐

Practiced self-compassion ☐

Engaged in pleasurable activities and hobbies ☐

Sought meaning and purpose in my life ☐

RELATIONAL CARE

Told people close to me why they were important ☐

Established or maintained healthy limits when necessary ☐

Let go of being "right" ☐

Took a nonjudgmental stance toward others ☐

Practiced empathy ☐

Spent time with people I care about ☐

SPIRITUAL CARE

Attended religious or spiritual services ☐

Spent time with others who have similar beliefs and goals ☐

Practiced mindfulness or meditated ☐

Prayed or asked others to pray for me ☐

Read or watched things that inspire me ☐

Honored my own values ☐

THIS WEEK...

I CREATED MORE HAPPINESS IN MY LIFE BY

I AM MOST THANKFUL FOR

I FOUND PEACE OF MIND IN

ENABLING

When we think of enabling, we can ask ourselves, "Am I doing something for my family member or loved one that they could do for themselves with a little bit of extra help, encouragement, and support?" But it isn't just family members who may be enabling. Therapists can also make that mistake.

One day an adolescent client asked me to advocate for her. She was just about to start driving and wanted to be allowed to drive a distance of about 100 miles to meet a friend who had moved away. This client was very responsible and even a bit too cautious, so I was in full support of a goal that encouraged more independence and yet mom and dad needed to make the final decision.

I was just about to say, "Of course I'll talk to your parents!" but then I stopped. I could easily do an effective DEAR MAN (a DBT skill to help us get what we want) but that didn't help my client to advocate for herself. Since self-advocacy is something she'll do for the rest of her life, it's a good thing for her to start practicing at the age of 16.

So before I made a big mistake, I asked the client to start the DEAR MAN skill and told her that I was happy to edit or make suggestions once she made the first draft.

But jumping in and problem-solving or helping someone else comes from a good place. It's done out of unconditional love and concern. You wouldn't be doing it if you didn't care.

It may also be challenging, though, to figure out what your family member is capable of.

If you know (or strongly suspect) that your loved one cannot do something and needs help, then you'll probably want to do whatever you can until they do have the skills to solve a particular problem. If they are open to being taught, then you want to do that in a way that is gentle and doesn't increase any shame or guilt.

It might be helpful, if you have your family member's permission, to make a call or send an email to their therapist to say, "Kayla is overdrawn at the bank again. I think that she may need some extra help when it comes to tolerating her distress when it comes to staying within her weekly budget." You're not tattling nor are you judging; you're merely providing additional information. While this can worth with children and adolescents, it may not be as effective (nor appropriate) with adults.

When it comes to things that your family member or friend can do for themselves, please be very cautious with what may amount to more than an occasional kind act. It's important to recognize that your loved one desperately needs the self-respect and dignity that comes with helping himself or herself whenever and wherever they can.

You also want to be very careful in making decisions about how you want to expend your energy. If you are continually rescuing or doing too much too often, you'll find that you're quickly burned out. People with BPD need healthy role models who are practicing good self-care and demonstrate healthy limits with others. Saving others from the consequences of their voluntary actions over and over again is a habit you don't need.

Remember that it's okay to put on your own oxygen mask before you help anyone else. In fact, it's more than okay. It's essential.

FOR THIS WEEK

Consider how much you are going above and beyond to help your loved one.

Are you helping them to become healthier, happier, and more independent or is the extra assistance potentially holding them back?

CHECKLIST

Check all that you accomplished (or plan to accomplish) this week.

PHYSICAL CARE

Exercised 4-6 times ☐

Balanced sleep ☐

Paid attention to nutrition ☐

Ate mindfully ☐

Used alcohol in moderation ☐

Did not self-medicate ☐

EMOTIONAL CARE

Asked for help ☐

Went to individual or family therapy ☐

Made time for enjoyable activities ☐

Practiced self-compassion ☐

Engaged in pleasurable activities and hobbies ☐

Sought meaning and purpose in my life ☐

RELATIONAL CARE

Told people close to me why they were important ☐

Established or maintained healthy limits when necessary ☐

Let go of being "right" ☐

Took a nonjudgmental stance toward others ☐

Practiced empathy ☐

Spent time with people I care about ☐

SPIRITUAL CARE

Attended religious or spiritual services ☐

Spent time with others who have similar beliefs and goals ☐

Practiced mindfulness or meditated ☐

Prayed or asked others to pray for me ☐

Read or watched things that inspire me ☐

Honored my own values ☐

THIS WEEK...

I CREATED MORE HAPPINESS IN MY LIFE BY

I AM MOST THANKFUL FOR

I FOUND PEACE OF MIND IN

MONTHLY

SELF-CARE ASSESSMENT

Over the past 28 days, how often have you engaged in these specific self-care methods?

PHYSICAL CARE	SCORE
Exercised 4–6 times a week	
Balanced sleep	
Paid attention to nutrition	
Ate mindfully	
Used alcohol in moderation	
Did not self-medicate	

TOTAL SCORE FOR THIS SECTION

EMOTIONAL CARE	SCORE
Asked for help	
Went to individual or family therapy	
Made time for enjoyable activities	
Practiced self-compassion	
Engaged in pleasurable activities and hobbies	
Sought meaning and purpose in my life	

TOTAL SCORE FOR THIS SECTION

TOTAL SCORE PER SECTION

20-24	**Excellent!** You're doing a great job of taking care of yourself in this area.
15-19	**Very good.** Identify and address any gaps in self-care.
BELOW 15	**No one is perfect.** Is this an area of growth for you?

Remember, a score of zero (not applicable) in any area may lower your section score.

RELATIONAL CARE	SCORE
Told people close to me why they were important	
Established or maintained healthy limits when necessary	
Let go of being "right"	
Took a nonjudgmental stance toward others	
Practiced empathy	
Spent time with people I care about	

TOTAL SCORE FOR THIS SECTION

SPIRITUAL CARE	SCORE
Attended religious or spiritual services	
Spent time with others who have similar beliefs and goals	
Practiced mindfulness or meditated	
Prayed or asked others to pray for me	
Read or watched things that inspire me	
Honored my own values	

TOTAL SCORE FOR THIS SECTION

HOW TO LET BPD RUIN YOUR LIFE

Sometimes people with BPD allow their symptoms to take over their lives. Family members and friends can also be guilty of making life more difficult and complicated both for themselves and the individual in their life with BPD.

Below are some thoughts about how you might voluntarily be ruining your own life.

(It might also be true that someone else in the family is engaging in these behaviors even if you aren't.)

1. IGNORE YOUR OWN NEEDS

One of the best ways for you to make things much more difficult is to ignore, suppress, or be dismissive of your own emotional, physical, financial, and spiritual needs. If you've planned a fun vacation or family event, you'll be the first one to cancel those plans because your loved one has a crisis and needs you. Accepting that unrelenting crises or emergencies are a part of ordinary life means that you delay honoring your own needs for weeks, months, years, or even decades.

The same is true for your financial needs. If you are saving for retirement or other important goals, you might consider setting aside those needs as well.

2. DON'T SEEK SUPPORT

You might think that most families get by with very little or no support or encouragement. They figure things out all on their own, or maybe they pretend that everything is just fine or that they'll get better all on their own.

Loved ones of individuals with BPD can help ruin their lives by refusing to seek help or their therapy, or you might wait until your own emotional or physical health is at risk before you begin to take these needs seriously. When in doubt, you ignore or push away thoughts that you might also need help.

3. IMAGINE THAT YOU HAVE CONTROL OVER WHAT YOUR LOVED ONE DOES OR SAYS

Perhaps you and your family are that different from everyone else. When someone brings up the idea that ultimately you only have control over what you say or do, tell them that they're wrong. Maybe you are the person in your family member's life who will change them without any effort on their part.

It doesn't matter that your past attempts haven't been successful. You stubbornly decide to keep trying to change others for many more years.

4. CULTIVATE ANGER

Spend a lot of your days thinking about how life should be or how unfair life can be for you or your family member. Rage at doctors, therapists, health care systems, insurance companies, or God when things don't happen the way you thought. Decide that if you complain loudly and often things might change for you or your loved one.

To keep anger going, eschew as much responsibility as possible for your happiness and blame others as often as you can.

5. GIVE UP.

Firmly make up your mind that nothing will ever change for your family. You'll be the family that doesn't make it. You'll be the family who is always suffering. Think about all that you've already endured and don't allow yourself to hope that the future might be very different for your loved one.

FOR THIS WEEK

Be honest with yourself as to whether you are the family member who might be making things worse. Remember that individuals faced with a mental health diagnosis need positive role models who are taking care of themselves first. It's okay for you to work towards your own life worth living.

37

CHECKLIST

Check all that you accomplished
(or plan to accomplish) this week.

PHYSICAL CARE

Exercised 4-6 times ☐

Balanced sleep ☐

Paid attention to nutrition ☐

Ate mindfully ☐

Used alcohol in moderation ☐

Did not self-medicate ☐

EMOTIONAL CARE

Asked for help ☐

Went to individual or family therapy ☐

Made time for enjoyable activities ☐

Practiced self-compassion ☐

Engaged in pleasurable activities and hobbies ☐

Sought meaning and purpose in my life ☐

RELATIONAL CARE

Told people close to me why they were important ☐

Established or maintained healthy limits when necessary ☐

Let go of being "right" ☐

Took a nonjudgmental stance toward others ☐

Practiced empathy ☐

Spent time with people I care about ☐

SPIRITUAL CARE

Attended religious or spiritual services ☐

Spent time with others who have similar beliefs and goals ☐

Practiced mindfulness or meditated ☐

Prayed or asked others to pray for me ☐

Read or watched things that inspire me ☐

Honored my own values ☐

THIS WEEK...

I CREATED MORE
HAPPINESS IN MY LIFE BY

I AM MOST
THANKFUL FOR

I FOUND PEACE
OF MIND IN

WHAT'S THE FUNCTION OF THE BEHAVIOR?

Instead of complaining about others' behaviors we can imagine that there is a reason why people are behaving the way that they do.

FOR INSTANCE:

- People often cry as a way of communicating to others that they are in distress but it can also be an act that helps individuals to soothe themselves
- Yelling or screaming communicates our anger and tells others that an important goal is being blocked or that a value is being ignored
- Physical avoidance or wanting to be alone may communicate sadness, shame, or guilt to others
- Using drugs or alcohol can make sense when an individual wants to change the way they think or feel for a short time
- Ignoring responsibilities or everyday tasks of adulthood often indicates fear rather than apathy
- Suicidal thinking or planning tells others that life is wholly unacceptable in the way it's currently lived

Most of the time, instead of being curious about why people do the things that they do, we get judgmental or frustrated. We might think that others are doing these things to us and that it's personal.

WE MIGHT TELL OURSELVES:

- "She's making me angry." Instead of "Her actions are making me angry."
- "He doesn't care about others or he wouldn't be doing this again and again." Instead of "I'd love to understand why this keeps happening when we've asked him to stop."
- "She has the skills to make this work. If she doesn't use them right now, she's going to ruin our vacation." Instead of "There's a reason why she's not using her skills; we just don't have the missing piece to understanding why just yet."

There's often something we're telling ourselves that keeps us from feeling stuck in our own emotions. When we are stuck in our feelings, we make for ineffective parents, siblings, friends, children, and even therapists.

Being genuinely curious helps us most of the time. Playing the detective and brainstorming ideas about why people behave the way that they do usually get us closer to understanding and (here's the good part!) understanding is right around the corner from problem-solving.

FOR THIS WEEK

My challenge to you this week is to adopt a curious mindset that allows you the freedom to see your family member's behavior in a slightly different way.

38

CHECKLIST

Check all that you accomplished (or plan to accomplish) this week.

PHYSICAL CARE

- Exercised 4–6 times ☐
- Balanced sleep ☐
- Paid attention to nutrition ☐
- Ate mindfully ☐
- Used alcohol in moderation ☐
- Did not self-medicate ☐

EMOTIONAL CARE

- Asked for help ☐
- Went to individual or family therapy ☐
- Made time for enjoyable activities ☐
- Practiced self-compassion ☐
- Engaged in pleasurable activities and hobbies ☐
- Sought meaning and purpose in my life ☐

RELATIONAL CARE

- Told people close to me why they were important ☐
- Established or maintained healthy limits when necessary ☐
- Let go of being "right" ☐
- Took a nonjudgmental stance toward others ☐
- Practiced empathy ☐
- Spent time with people I care about ☐

SPIRITUAL CARE

- Attended religious or spiritual services ☐
- Spent time with others who have similar beliefs and goals ☐
- Practiced mindfulness or meditated ☐
- Prayed or asked others to pray for me ☐
- Read or watched things that inspire me ☐
- Honored my own values ☐

THIS WEEK...

I CREATED MORE HAPPINESS IN MY LIFE BY

I AM MOST THANKFUL FOR

I FOUND PEACE OF MIND IN

A DIALECTIC OF RECOVERY

Within DBT we strive for the synthesis of opposing views and ideas. That synthesis is most commonly referred to as Wise Mind.

Wise Mind is a place where we are acting neither out of emotion nor logic. We honor both but cling to neither. It's here where we begin to let go of some of our black-and-white thinking and find room for a middle path. You already know that this is a much healthier place to live.

For me, there have been two opposing views of recovery over the past decade:

- Work hard to get better fast; and
- Be patient.

Finding the dialectic between the two has been challenging.

WORK HARD TO GET BETTER FAST

People who don't skip therapy appointments, consistently reach out and ask for help, and put their recovery first will see some pretty significant (and lasting) results anywhere between six and twelve months. While treatment may require a significant commitment, making an investment in an evidence-based treatment like DBT can yield great returns.

This same idea is true for any goal we set in life. The harder we work, the more results we'll see. The greater the effort, the richer our reward. Hard work really does pay off in treatment.

BE PATIENT

The other side of working really hard to get better in the fastest time frame possible is to be patient.

Being patient means taking the time (even if it takes years) to figure out what works, what doesn't, and how we can from our mistakes. We learn from failure in a way that we do not learn from our successes.

Patience also teaches us an important lesson in watching life unfold in just the way it was meant to transpire.

THE DIALECTIC

Even though we'd like for things to be different, recovery simply doesn't happen in a nice linear and predictable way. It's usually full of encouraging starts, disappointing stops, and progress that can sometimes be challenging to spot even on the best of days.

People with a diagnosis of BPD are often under a great deal of pressure to change quickly. For example, spouses may threaten divorce or well-meaning parents may insist that their child return to college shortly after a suicide attempt. For some people, these may be effective motivators for change but for others it will only be an impediment that will stall recovery.

The secret is in honoring the dialectic between pushing for hard work and being exceptionally patient with someone you love. The bigger secret is to know when to push and when to practice patience.

FOR THIS WEEK

When is it best to be patient and when is it more appropriate to gently nudge toward change?

CHECKLIST

Check all that you accomplished
(or plan to accomplish) this week.

PHYSICAL CARE

Exercised 4-6 times ☐

Balanced sleep ☐

Paid attention to nutrition ☐

Ate mindfully ☐

Used alcohol in moderation ☐

Did not self-medicate ☐

EMOTIONAL CARE

Asked for help ☐

Went to individual or family therapy ☐

Made time for enjoyable activities ☐

Practiced self-compassion ☐

Engaged in pleasurable activities and hobbies ☐

Sought meaning and purpose in my life ☐

RELATIONAL CARE

Told people close to me why they were important ☐

Established or maintained healthy limits when necessary ☐

Let go of being "right" ☐

Took a nonjudgmental stance toward others ☐

Practiced empathy ☐

Spent time with people I care about ☐

SPIRITUAL CARE

Attended religious or spiritual services ☐

Spent time with others who have similar beliefs and goals ☐

Practiced mindfulness or meditated ☐

Prayed or asked others to pray for me ☐

Read or watched things that inspire me ☐

Honored my own values ☐

THIS WEEK...

I CREATED MORE HAPPINESS IN MY LIFE BY

I AM MOST THANKFUL FOR

I FOUND PEACE OF MIND IN

VALIDATION IS (RARELY) ENOUGH

Validation means that we are acknowledging another person's emotions, thoughts, or experiences. Consistent and heart-felt validation communicates, "I know how you are feeling and I care about what is happening."

For most people who have a mental health diagnosis, that validation is an invitation to re-regulate our emotions. Being understood is calming. When we are calm, we're almost always in a place where we can make good decisions about what happens next.

For instance, when your loved one feels validated, they are so much less likely to hurt themselves or others. They are much less likely to get in their way and self-sabotage.

I started to title this week "Validation isn't Enough" but then changed it to "Validation is (Rarely) Enough." It's true that for some of my clients, validation can be enough. Once they are validated by the people they care about the most, they can soothe themselves or problem-solve. This is especially true for individuals who have reached a particular place in their recovery or for those who already have a lot of coping skills in place. They are saying, "I may have needed a jump start, but I can take it from here."

However, most people with BPD will need more than validation. Validation gets the ball rolling but it must also be meet with motivation to change, problem-solving, and often some uncomfortable reminders about natural, adult consequences.

A very abbreviated version of the two approaches might look like something like this:

Young adult: I hate this professor. She already hates me. If I stay in this class, I'll fail. I have to drop out. I can't stand it.

Parent: You've had such a rough start to the semester. I know that you were looking forward to taking this class.

Young adult: I know, but I can't do it. I can't stand it.

Parent: You're so close to graduating. I'd hate to see you stop now. I wonder how we can help you make it through this class.

Young adult: I don't know. I don't see how it's possible.

Parent: I have some ideas but, honestly, I don't want to tell you what to do. Maybe we can figure it out together so that you can still graduate on time.

Young adult: Maybe.

Now I certainly understand that conversations rarely come together in quite this way, but it's also true that things can come together quickly and easily. You may need to keep validating until your family member is ready to take that next step with you. A gentle push or a reminder about real world consequences (this isn't the same as issuing ultimatums or being punishing) is almost always necessary when it comes to helping someone you love take that next step towards helping themselves.

Validation isn't magic, but it can be an effective tool so that your loved one can reach their own goals of having a life worth living.

FOR THIS WEEK

This week I'd love for you to become more aware of how and when you are practicing validation.

Are you stopping too soon and giving up or are you finding a way to motivate your family member?

CHECKLIST

Check all that you accomplished
(or plan to accomplish) this week.

PHYSICAL CARE

Exercised 4–6 times ☐

Balanced sleep ☐

Paid attention to nutrition ☐

Ate mindfully ☐

Used alcohol in moderation ☐

Did not self-medicate ☐

EMOTIONAL CARE

Asked for help ☐

Went to individual or family therapy ☐

Made time for enjoyable activities ☐

Practiced self-compassion ☐

Engaged in pleasurable activities and hobbies ☐

Sought meaning and purpose in my life ☐

RELATIONAL CARE

Told people close to me why they were important ☐

Established or maintained healthy limits when necessary ☐

Let go of being "right" ☐

Took a nonjudgmental stance toward others ☐

Practiced empathy ☐

Spent time with people I care about ☐

SPIRITUAL CARE

Attended religious or spiritual services ☐

Spent time with others who have similar beliefs and goals ☐

Practiced mindfulness or meditated ☐

Prayed or asked others to pray for me ☐

Read or watched things that inspire me ☐

Honored my own values ☐

THIS WEEK...

I CREATED MORE HAPPINESS IN MY LIFE BY

I AM MOST THANKFUL FOR

I FOUND PEACE OF MIND IN

MONTHLY
SELF-CARE ASSESSMENT

Over the past 28 days, how often have you engaged in these specific self-care methods?

PHYSICAL CARE	SCORE
Exercised 4–6 times a week	
Balanced sleep	
Paid attention to nutrition	
Ate mindfully	
Used alcohol in moderation	
Did not self-medicate	

TOTAL SCORE FOR THIS SECTION

EMOTIONAL CARE	SCORE
Asked for help	
Went to individual or family therapy	
Made time for enjoyable activities	
Practiced self-compassion	
Engaged in pleasurable activities and hobbies	
Sought meaning and purpose in my life	

TOTAL SCORE FOR THIS SECTION

TOTAL SCORE PER SECTION

20-24	**Excellent!** You're doing a great job of taking care of yourself in this area.
15-19	**Very good.** Identify and address any gaps in self-care.
BELOW 15	**No one is perfect.** Is this an area of growth for you?

Remember, a score of zero (not applicable) in any area may lower your section score.

RELATIONAL CARE	SCORE
Told people close to me why they were important	
Established or maintained healthy limits when necessary	
Let go of being "right"	
Took a nonjudgmental stance toward others	
Practiced empathy	
Spent time with people I care about	

TOTAL SCORE FOR THIS SECTION

SPIRITUAL CARE	SCORE
Attended religious or spiritual services	
Spent time with others who have similar beliefs and goals	
Practiced mindfulness or meditated	
Prayed or asked others to pray for me	
Read or watched things that inspire me	
Honored my own values	

TOTAL SCORE FOR THIS SECTION

SCHEMAS

People with BPD often get stuck believing things that other people do not, or they may think things that are just not accurate. These schemas are ideas that endure month after month or year after year. They don't go away after just a little bit of treatment or a flash of insight.

They often persist even after contradictory evidence has been presented. There's also a treatment for BPD centered around identifying and challenging schemas.

For people with BPD, it's extraordinarily common to think things like:

- I am unworthy.
- I am a victim.
- I cannot control my behavior.
- Life isn't worth living.
- I cannot trust others.
- I will always get hurt.
- I cannot recover.
- I will never be happy.

These types of beliefs interfere with your family member's ability to create a healthier and happier life.

Now your loved one may not be verbalizing these ideas, but they still might be there. You might even have your own schemas that you can identify in your own life.

As someone in recovery, I remember thinking for the longest time that everyone important in my life would go away if I recovered. I was convinced that people would think that I could always solve my own problems and that they'd stop calling and asking me if I was okay.

Because I was always in crisis, I got the message that people loved me because they'd rush to my side every time I fell apart. As you can imagine, this created a situation where some of these behaviors were inadvertently reinforced (or rewarded) by the responses of others.

I hate to admit this, but sometimes I'd even manufacture a crisis just so that I could be assured that people cared about me.

Of course, what I needed the most was for people to call me and express an interest in my life when I wasn't in crisis because that did two things:

- stopped the reinforcement because I didn't need to be having a tantrum nor did I need to be in the middle of a mess to know that people cared and loved me
- provided me with evidence that my schema ("People will leave if I'm better or can solve my problems.") was incorrect

It took a long time for me to understand what healthy relationships looked like. I couldn't comprehend that sometimes limits (my limits or the limits that others imposed) could be healthy choices in relationships. I learned that I didn't have to be in a crisis to get others to pay attention to me.

Instead of being ignored as I moved forward in recovery, I got to see how people wanted to be around me a little more. Amazingly, when I liked myself more, I found that others also liked me.

One by one, my schemas were shattered, and I had the freedom to think dialectically and be more flexible in how I understood how the world worked. My black-and-white thinking was no longer entirely so black-or-white or all-or-nothing all the time.

Understanding how your loved one thinks can help you to respond to those ideas with assurance, love, and (always) validation.

FOR THIS WEEK

Consider the schemas that your friend or family member may be holding onto.

What kind of ideas do they believe today about themselves and the world?

CHECKLIST

Check all that you accomplished (or plan to accomplish) this week.

PHYSICAL CARE

Exercised 4–6 times ☐

Balanced sleep ☐

Paid attention to nutrition ☐

Ate mindfully ☐

Used alcohol in moderation ☐

Did not self-medicate ☐

EMOTIONAL CARE

Asked for help ☐

Went to individual or family therapy ☐

Made time for enjoyable activities ☐

Practiced self-compassion ☐

Engaged in pleasurable activities and hobbies ☐

Sought meaning and purpose in my life ☐

RELATIONAL CARE

Told people close to me why they were important ☐

Established or maintained healthy limits when necessary ☐

Let go of being "right" ☐

Took a nonjudgmental stance toward others ☐

Practiced empathy ☐

Spent time with people I care about ☐

SPIRITUAL CARE

Attended religious or spiritual services ☐

Spent time with others who have similar beliefs and goals ☐

Practiced mindfulness or meditated ☐

Prayed or asked others to pray for me ☐

Read or watched things that inspire me ☐

Honored my own values ☐

THIS WEEK...

I CREATED MORE HAPPINESS IN MY LIFE BY

I AM MOST THANKFUL FOR

I FOUND PEACE OF MIND IN

YOU ARE A ROLE MODEL

Most of the learning we encounter in life is done in a social context. We learn by watching others. For individuals with BPD, we often wind up imitating the behavior of others we are around.

At any given moments, our behaviors are being shaped by those around us.

I've seen this in my DBT skills training group for years on end now. Most people come into a group not knowing what to do or say. They quickly learn, however, when they follow the examples of others who have been in the group longer and seem a little more confident and relaxed.

The message they are getting is, "Do this, and you'll be okay." For the most part, this winds up being a positive experience and is often the first step to developing healthier relationships and even establishing friendships.

But you are one of the most influential role models for your family member or friend. How you control your anger makes a difference. How you validate makes a difference. How you forgive or hold grudges makes a difference. How you speak with compassion about others makes a difference. How you take care of your emotional health makes a difference.

Simply put, what you do affects your loved one and what they do affects you.

Now you have very little control (or absolutely no control) over what your family member does or says but you do have control to change your behavior.

A long time ago, I was working with an adolescent who was thrown into a suicidal crisis whenever her dad lost control over his emotions to the point where he appeared to be on the cusp of physical violence. The dad never harmed anyone in his family but what looked like an imminent threat was effective in getting my client to think that she should no longer be alive for days at a time. Understanding the pattern made a difference for my client but getting dad the tools he needed to manage his own emotions was even more critical. As a result, my client had significantly fewer suicidal crises, and the family relationship improved.

This doesn't mean that one person has the power to "cure" another person but it would be a mistake to think that we aren't in a position to make a positive and lasting difference with every person we come in contact with today—even if it's for just a brief moment or two. We really do learn from watching others. We can build others up, or our actions can tear others down.

When one person begins to change, the family system changes.

It's tempting to sit back and imagine that our actions don't matter or that we'll just be ignored or dismissed. Many family members I work with feel that way. Sometimes I still think that way, too.

EVEN WHEN YOU DON'T THINK THAT YOU'RE MAKING A DIFFERENCE, PLEASE KNOW THAT YOU ARE

FOR THIS WEEK

Think about how your behaviors make a helpful (or not-so-helpful) difference for your emotionally sensitive loved one.

Who else in your world is being impacted by the things you do or say?

CHECKLIST

Check all that you accomplished (or plan to accomplish) this week.

PHYSICAL CARE

Exercised 4-6 times ☐

Balanced sleep ☐

Paid attention to nutrition ☐

Ate mindfully ☐

Used alcohol in moderation ☐

Did not self-medicate ☐

EMOTIONAL CARE

Asked for help ☐

Went to individual or family therapy ☐

Made time for enjoyable activities ☐

Practiced self-compassion ☐

Engaged in pleasurable activities and hobbies ☐

Sought meaning and purpose in my life ☐

RELATIONAL CARE

Told people close to me why they were important ☐

Established or maintained healthy limits when necessary ☐

Let go of being "right" ☐

Took a nonjudgmental stance toward others ☐

Practiced empathy ☐

Spent time with people I care about ☐

SPIRITUAL CARE

Attended religious or spiritual services ☐

Spent time with others who have similar beliefs and goals ☐

Practiced mindfulness or meditated ☐

Prayed or asked others to pray for me ☐

Read or watched things that inspire me ☐

Honored my own values ☐

THIS WEEK...

I CREATED MORE HAPPINESS IN MY LIFE BY

I AM MOST THANKFUL FOR

I FOUND PEACE OF MIND IN

ALTERNATIVE THERAPIES AND TREATMENTS

Occasionally I'll get a question about alternative therapies or treatments for BPD. Do they work? Are they effective? Are they better than no treatment at all for clients who want to take a different approach to their recovery?

Alternative therapies may include creative therapies (such as art, dance, and music), physical or body therapies (walk and talk therapy, hippotherapy, yoga, massage, and wilderness therapy), trauma (EMDR or exposure treatment), and novel pharmaceutical approaches such as ketamine have become popular over the past several years for reducing suicidal thinking and planning within hours of administration. Support groups and self-help organizations (such as NAMI's Peer-to-Peer program or Alcoholics Anonymous) might also be included in a list of alternative or complementary treatments.

One day I received a call from a mother who was looking for an alternative treatment for her son who was in his early 20s. He wasn't interested in DBT and was looking for solutions that also included psychedelics or marijuana. While I want to be open about alternative treatments, at this time, we have no research to support the use of this type of approach for individuals who are looking to reduce the symptoms related to BPD outside of anecdotal evidence.

In fact, we have very little or no evidence to suggest that any alternative or complementary therapies can make a difference in helping people with the core symptoms of BPD. That's not to say that art therapy, massages, or a structured support group can't help people with BPD but I want to be very careful about recommending an approach that is not backed by research—especially for individuals with BPD who are engaging in life-threatening behaviors or are addicted to alcohol or drugs.

Ideally, all of my consulting and therapy clients would have a wide variety of effective treatment options available to them wherever they may live. Unfortunately, the reality is that even in larger cities in the United States, excellent treatment options may be limited by waiting lists, cost, or other factors.

Since there is no "perfect" treatment, I encourage all of my clients (or potential clients) to make a list of pros and cons when it comes to deciding on what might be best for them. I believe that the question, "Is there research to show that this is helpful for people with BPD?" is crucial but there are certainly other important considerations.

For most people, effective treatment will be one of the best investments they'll make in their lives. As you can imagine, I want all of my clients (and their families) to have as much information as possible so that they can make smart health care decisions.

FOR THIS WEEK

This week I'd love for you to consider what kind of treatment or treatment approach has been most helpful for your family member. What has made the biggest difference in their life?

CHECKLIST

Check all that you accomplished
(or plan to accomplish) this week.

PHYSICAL CARE

Exercised 4–6 times ☐

Balanced sleep ☐

Paid attention to nutrition ☐

Ate mindfully ☐

Used alcohol in moderation ☐

Did not self-medicate ☐

EMOTIONAL CARE

Asked for help ☐

Went to individual or family therapy ☐

Made time for enjoyable activities ☐

Practiced self-compassion ☐

Engaged in pleasurable activities and hobbies ☐

Sought meaning and purpose in my life ☐

RELATIONAL CARE

Told people close to me why they were important ☐

Established or maintained healthy limits when necessary ☐

Let go of being "right" ☐

Took a nonjudgmental stance toward others ☐

Practiced empathy ☐

Spent time with people I care about ☐

SPIRITUAL CARE

Attended religious or spiritual services ☐

Spent time with others who have similar beliefs and goals ☐

Practiced mindfulness or meditated ☐

Prayed or asked others to pray for me ☐

Read or watched things that inspire me ☐

Honored my own values ☐

THIS WEEK...

I CREATED MORE HAPPINESS IN MY LIFE BY

I AM MOST THANKFUL FOR

I FOUND PEACE OF MIND IN

COPING AHEAD

If you've ever found yourself to be in the same challenging situation over and over again with someone you love, this DBT skill might be helpful to you.

YOU MIGHT DECIDE TO CREATE A COPING AHEAD PLAN FOR

- anger outbursts
- suicidal threats
- treatment failures or dropping out of treatment prematurely
- financial emergencies
- break-ups or divorce
- potential homelessness

You could also create a coping ahead plan for upcoming events such as vacations, family reunions, weddings, or family get-togethers.

HERE'S AN EXAMPLE FROM A PARENT'S PERSPECTIVE OF AN ONGOING PROBLEM:

1. Describe the situation. Be factual and let go of judgments.

My daughter has a tantrum and makes a threat that she is going to kill herself. If she leaves the house feeling suicidal, I don't have control over what happens next.

I'm terrified of what may happen if she gets in her car.

2. Describe the coping or problem-solving skills you would like to use.

DBT skills to use:

- Validation for her ("You must be feeling really desperate if you are thinking about hurting yourself," and self-validation for me "This is scary!")
- Letting go of judgment ("This shouldn't be happening!" or "Here we go again!")
- Wise Mind ("We're both doing the best we can right now, and we both have a lot of room for improvement.")
- Mindfulness (go to the bathroom, shut the door, and breathe mindfully for three minutes)
- DEAR MAN to help facilitate problem-solving ("I seem to be saying all the wrong things right now. What do you need from me?")
- DEAR MAN for when I need to ask for extra help (calling nonjudgmental friends, family members, counselor, etc.)

3. Imagine that you are in the situation. What are you thinking and feeling? What are your goals?

- I want for her to be physically safe. That will mean that she doesn't leave the house until she's back in Wise Mind.
- Am I choosing to be "right" over being effective and doing what works?
- The only one I can control at this moment is me.

4. Rehearse in your mind how you are coping effectively.

I am committing to be skillful.

I know that when I get upset, my daughter also gets upset. I can help both of us by staying in Wise Mind and doing whatever I can not to make a bad situation worse.

I will take ownership of my actions. That may mean apologizing and being vulnerable ("I hate it when I get so upset and yell like I just did. Will you forgive me for making things worse this afternoon?").

Now that you've got your plan, you need to use it for it to work.

Many family members keep emergency information (like their coping ahead plans) in a binder or on their phone in an app like Dropbox. Having your plan on your phone means that you can access it anywhere and at any time.

5. Use relaxation strategies once you've developed your coping ahead plan.

Problem-solving can be extraordinarily stressful. You may experience a sense of relief when you develop your coping ahead plan, but your anxiety might also remain reasonably high.

Finding ways to relax may help you cope with your own intense emotions.

FOR THIS WEEK

Have you developed your coping ahead plan?
If so, I'd love to know how beneficial
it was to you.

CHECKLIST

Check all that you accomplished
(or plan to accomplish) this week.

PHYSICAL CARE

Exercised 4-6 times ☐

Balanced sleep ☐

Paid attention to nutrition ☐

Ate mindfully ☐

Used alcohol in moderation ☐

Did not self-medicate ☐

EMOTIONAL CARE

Asked for help ☐

Went to individual or family therapy ☐

Made time for enjoyable activities ☐

Practiced self-compassion ☐

Engaged in pleasurable activities and hobbies ☐

Sought meaning and purpose in my life ☐

RELATIONAL CARE

Told people close to me why they were important ☐

Established or maintained healthy limits when necessary ☐

Let go of being "right" ☐

Took a nonjudgmental stance toward others ☐

Practiced empathy ☐

Spent time with people I care about ☐

SPIRITUAL CARE

Attended religious or spiritual services ☐

Spent time with others who have similar beliefs and goals ☐

Practiced mindfulness or meditated ☐

Prayed or asked others to pray for me ☐

Read or watched things that inspire me ☐

Honored my own values ☐

THIS WEEK...

I CREATED MORE HAPPINESS IN MY LIFE BY

I AM MOST THANKFUL FOR

I FOUND PEACE OF MIND IN

MONTHLY

SELF-CARE ASSESSMENT

Over the past 28 days, how often have you engaged in these specific self-care methods?

SCORING

4	**Always**
3	**Often**
2	**Sometimes**
1	**Rarely**
0	Not applicable to me at this time

PHYSICAL CARE	SCORE
Exercised 4–6 times a week	
Balanced sleep	
Paid attention to nutrition	
Ate mindfully	
Used alcohol in moderation	
Did not self-medicate	

TOTAL SCORE FOR THIS SECTION

EMOTIONAL CARE	SCORE
Asked for help	
Went to individual or family therapy	
Made time for enjoyable activities	
Practiced self-compassion	
Engaged in pleasurable activities and hobbies	
Sought meaning and purpose in my life	

TOTAL SCORE FOR THIS SECTION

TOTAL SCORE PER SECTION

20-24	**Excellent!** You're doing a great job of taking care of yourself in this area.
15-19	**Very good.** Identify and address any gaps in self-care.
BELOW 15	**No one is perfect.** Is this an area of growth for you?

Remember, a score of zero (not applicable) in any area may lower your section score.

RELATIONAL CARE	SCORE
Told people close to me why they were important	
Established or maintained healthy limits when necessary	
Let go of being "right"	
Took a nonjudgmental stance toward others	
Practiced empathy	
Spent time with people I care about	

TOTAL SCORE FOR THIS SECTION ⬚

SPIRITUAL CARE	SCORE
Attended religious or spiritual services	
Spent time with others who have similar beliefs and goals	
Practiced mindfulness or meditated	
Prayed or asked others to pray for me	
Read or watched things that inspire me	
Honored my own values	

TOTAL SCORE FOR THIS SECTION ⬚

WEEK 45

A SENSE OF IDENTITY

Several weeks ago, I was working with a skeptical family member who was trying hard to understand Dialectical Behavior Therapy. He wanted to go slowly through the symptoms of BPD and match up the potential corresponding skills from DBT.

Then it came time to talk about having a sense of identity, self-image, and self-respect. When I noted that there wasn't necessarily a specific skill that we could use when there was a moment of personal uncertainty in his wife's life, he became concerned that DBT wouldn't be a good fit.

He insisted, "But this is a core part of BPD." And he's right.

It's extraordinarily common for people with BPD to feel lost in understanding who they are. Someone may point out a specific gift or talent, and we're enthusiastically off and running in one direction with great purpose. If someone else points out that achieving a particular goal will take X number of years or that not everyone will be successful then maybe we become discouraged and give up in a matter of days, weeks, or months.

Unfortunately, a sense of self or a strong identity makes for an ambiguous treatment goal, too. How do we know when we've arrived? How will we feel? Will we be bored? Empty? Will we feel accomplished and proud? What if we find out that we still don't love ourselves even after a lot of hard work?

I'd also suggest that there are a lot of different ways that we find our identities. Here are just a few:

RELATIONSHIPS

I feel like I have a strong identity in being a wife and sister, but there are also days when I feel the most fulfilled when I have a client who has done something brave and extraordinary. Healthy experiences through romantic love and friendship can be excellent catalysts for healing and recovery.

WORK

For me, work is definitely tied to having important relationships, but that's certainly not true for everyone. Without a doubt, I believe that meaningful (and paid) work is a core part of recovery because it increases our independence, alleviates boredom, and gives us something to do each day. Work also helps us to learn how to be accountable to others.

HOBBIES AND INTERESTS

Watching Netflix is not a hobby, but there are countless other ways for individuals with BPD to find a sense of self through engaging in enjoyable activities. I currently have a client who is teaching herself calligraphy. I might be biased, but I think that she's incredibly talented and her work has helped her to see that she has many different strengths.

FAITH AND RELIGION

Individuals with BPD may have different and challenging views about their faith, but for many people, this can be another area of life that helps us to see that we are not alone in our suffering. Finding ways to connect with others who share similar beliefs and values can help us to feel less lonely and provide us with the support and comfort we all seek.

It would be nice if there were one DBT skill or set of skills that help us to understand who we are but that just isn't the case.

Several years ago, I had a client who remarked, "I expect to work on me for the rest of my life." Maybe understanding who we are is an example of that challenging (and ongoing) work we're all called to do.

Giving up or insisting that there must be a more comfortable or faster way isn't the answer to greater self-awareness.

FOR THIS WEEK

Gently observe how your family member or loved one is creating that healthy self-identity.

What has been most helpful to them?

CHECKLIST

Check all that you accomplished (or plan to accomplish) this week.

PHYSICAL CARE

Exercised 4-6 times ☐

Balanced sleep ☐

Paid attention to nutrition ☐

Ate mindfully ☐

Used alcohol in moderation ☐

Did not self-medicate ☐

EMOTIONAL CARE

Asked for help ☐

Went to individual or family therapy ☐

Made time for enjoyable activities ☐

Practiced self-compassion ☐

Engaged in pleasurable activities and hobbies ☐

Sought meaning and purpose in my life ☐

RELATIONAL CARE

Told people close to me why they were important ☐

Established or maintained healthy limits when necessary ☐

Let go of being "right" ☐

Took a nonjudgmental stance toward others ☐

Practiced empathy ☐

Spent time with people I care about ☐

SPIRITUAL CARE

Attended religious or spiritual services ☐

Spent time with others who have similar beliefs and goals ☐

Practiced mindfulness or meditated ☐

Prayed or asked others to pray for me ☐

Read or watched things that inspire me ☐

Honored my own values ☐

THIS WEEK...

I CREATED MORE HAPPINESS IN MY LIFE BY

I AM MOST THANKFUL FOR

I FOUND PEACE OF MIND IN

IS BPD A "SEVERE" MENTAL ILLNESS?

At one time I had a client who got quite upset with me because I described BPD as a "severe" mental illness. She felt like it wasn't an accurate description of who she was and since then I've tried to be more mindful with the words I use to describe the disorder.

SO, I MIGHT TRY TO DIFFERENTIATE BETWEEN:

	More Severe Symptoms	Less Severe Symptoms
1	A diagnosis of BPD coupled with **chronic** drug and alcohol use	A diagnosis of BPD coupled with **only occasional or no** drug or alcohol use
2	A diagnosis of BPD with **frequent** hospital and emergency room visits	A diagnosis of BPD and **very few or no** hospital and emergency room visits
3	A diagnosis of BPD and **repeated failed attempts** to volunteer, attend school, or be employed for more extended periods of time	A diagnosis of BPD and **extended periods** of academic and vocational success
4	A diagnosis of BPD and **very few or no** meaningful relationships outside of the family	A diagnosis of BPD and **several positive,** meaningful relationships with people outside of the family
5	A diagnosis of BPD and **very poor** management of everyday stressors	A diagnosis of BPD and **moderate to good** management of ordinary stressful events
6	A diagnosis of BPD and **an inability** to accept personal responsibility for behaviors and choices	A diagnosis of BPD and **a healthier balance** between an acceptance of self and others
7	A diagnosis of BPD with **overwhelming** hopelessness, sadness, and despair about the future	A diagnosis of BPD, **a sense** of hopefulness and **a belief** in the ability to change, recover, and grow

Not everyone with a diagnosis of BPD is the same.
I invalidated my client by boxing her into a label that didn't fit or feel true to how she saw herself. Understanding how your loved one identifies with a diagnosis of BPD can be a key when it comes to opening the door to healthier communication.

FOR THIS WEEK

How do you think your loved one would describe themselves and the challenges they experience when it comes to their anxiety, depression, self-worth, and their ability to get along with others?

CHECKLIST

Check all that you accomplished
(or plan to accomplish) this week.

PHYSICAL CARE

Exercised 4–6 times ☐

Balanced sleep ☐

Paid attention to nutrition ☐

Ate mindfully ☐

Used alcohol in moderation ☐

Did not self-medicate ☐

EMOTIONAL CARE

Asked for help ☐

Went to individual or family therapy ☐

Made time for enjoyable activities ☐

Practiced self-compassion ☐

Engaged in pleasurable activities and hobbies ☐

Sought meaning and purpose in my life ☐

RELATIONAL CARE

Told people close to me why they were important ☐

Established or maintained healthy limits when necessary ☐

Let go of being "right" ☐

Took a nonjudgmental stance toward others ☐

Practiced empathy ☐

Spent time with people I care about ☐

SPIRITUAL CARE

Attended religious or spiritual services ☐

Spent time with others who have similar beliefs and goals ☐

Practiced mindfulness or meditated ☐

Prayed or asked others to pray for me ☐

Read or watched things that inspire me ☐

Honored my own values ☐

THIS WEEK...

I CREATED MORE HAPPINESS IN MY LIFE BY

I AM MOST THANKFUL FOR

I FOUND PEACE OF MIND IN

CATALYSTS FOR CHANGE

Nothing changes until something is different. This isn't merely true for your family member or friend with a mental health diagnosis, but it's also true for you. Think about the last time you made a change. **What was the catalyst? The spark?**

For many people, it's an internal voice urging us that we can eat better, be kinder, keep a cleaner home, try sobriety, or finally train for that 5k race.

For other people, the change may start due to an external factor. Perhaps a spouse has expressed concern about a particular habit, or a boss says that things need to must be done differently. Change may even be due to an event like an upcoming birthday, anniversary, or the fresh promise of a new year.

And change may be brought on by a combination of both internal and external reasons.

YOUR LOVED ONE WITH BPD IS NO DIFFERENT

For me, my reasons for changing were more internal than external. No one was necessarily urging me towards change. I wanted to be happier, and I was always seeing one therapist or another but talking about everyday problems week after week wasn't helping me to make lasting change in my life. There came a time when I knew that I'd have to do something different if I knew that I was going to get better.

But I also have many wonderful clients who have been actively encouraged by family members to seek treatment, and that seems to work, too. It's hard to sit in a DBT skills training group week after week and month after month and not learn anything at all.

You may have found a similar truth in your own life. Perhaps there was a class in college that you didn't particularly want to take but, in the end, you found that it was actually helpful or interesting. There are similar lessons to be learned every day if we're open to them.

What I do know is that change doesn't happen unless we are willing to try something different. That means that we must be ready to take a risk and be vulnerable. A new therapist or a new treatment program may be one more failure waiting to happen, or it may be that this time will be very, very different.

This next small change may spark the fire that leads you and your family to greater health and happiness.

I know that it can be tempting to give up or give in but now is not the time. Please don't believe that things are hopeless.

IT COULD BE THAT YOUR MIRACLE IS JUST STARTING TO TAKE SHAPE.

FOR THIS WEEK

Think about the last big change you made in your own life.

What were the factors behind that change?

What made a difference for you?

47

CHECKLIST

Check all that you accomplished
(or plan to accomplish) this week.

PHYSICAL CARE

Exercised 4-6 times ☐

Balanced sleep ☐

Paid attention to nutrition ☐

Ate mindfully ☐

Used alcohol in moderation ☐

Did not self-medicate ☐

EMOTIONAL CARE

Asked for help ☐

Went to individual or family therapy ☐

Made time for enjoyable activities ☐

Practiced self-compassion ☐

Engaged in pleasurable activities and hobbies ☐

Sought meaning and purpose in my life ☐

RELATIONAL CARE

Told people close to me why they were important ☐

Established or maintained healthy limits when necessary ☐

Let go of being "right" ☐

Took a nonjudgmental stance toward others ☐

Practiced empathy ☐

Spent time with people I care about ☐

SPIRITUAL CARE

Attended religious or spiritual services ☐

Spent time with others who have similar beliefs and goals ☐

Practiced mindfulness or meditated ☐

Prayed or asked others to pray for me ☐

Read or watched things that inspire me ☐

Honored my own values ☐

THIS WEEK...

I CREATED MORE HAPPINESS IN MY LIFE BY

I AM MOST THANKFUL FOR

I FOUND PEACE OF MIND IN

WEEK 48

EFFECTIVE COMMUNICATIONS

I believe that "I" statements (and evidence–based treatment) can save the world. They help us to effectively communicate about what is essential without judgment, threats, or accusations.

WHAT IS AN "I" STATEMENT? IT LOOKS LIKE THIS:

I feel… (state your emotion) when you…. (describe their behavior or under what conditions you feel this way) because… (explain why their behavior or the conditions cause you to feel this way).

HERE'S AN EXAMPLE FROM MY OWN THERAPY PRACTICE:

At one point I was working with a relatively new client who has been having a difficult time committing to treatment, and she'd missed most of her appointments. My client allowed me to speak with her parents one week and they told me that they didn't believe that their daughter was serious about treatment because the parents think that she's made it a habit of telling people what they want to hear instead of being honest. They didn't know if she was ready for the hard work that treatment requires.

While that might be true, if we are assuming that everyone is doing the best that they can at any given moment, there might be a different explanation for what's happening with their daughter. The parents may begin to understand more by starting off their conversation using an "I" statement.

REMEMBER:

The big goal is to get the daughter to make a commitment to therapy and not put their loved one in a position where she shuts down or gets immediately defensive.

WITH THAT IN MIND, THEIR "I" STATEMENT MAY LOOK LIKE THIS:

I feel afraid when you miss your therapy appointments because I hate to see you feeling so discouraged and hopeless.

or they might say:

I feel confused when you don't go to your scheduled appointments because you've told me that going to therapy was a priority for you this summer.

or even:

I feel sad when you don't go to your therapy appointments because I love you and want for you to feel better.

Your next step is to be very quiet and listen. It may be tempting to give advice, judge, scold, warn, or admonish but right now all you want to do is mindfully listen.

I suspect that you may be pleasantly surprised about how useful this communication strategy can be.

FOR THIS WEEK

No one uses "I" statements all the time. This is a skill that can be learned and practiced over an extended period. This week I'd love for you to practice an "I" statement just once. How does it feel for you to use it? How did your family member respond? Was it helpful for you or them?

48

CHECKLIST

Check all that you accomplished (or plan to accomplish) this week.

PHYSICAL CARE

Exercised 4–6 times ☐

Balanced sleep ☐

Paid attention to nutrition ☐

Ate mindfully ☐

Used alcohol in moderation ☐

Did not self-medicate ☐

EMOTIONAL CARE

Asked for help ☐

Went to individual or family therapy ☐

Made time for enjoyable activities ☐

Practiced self-compassion ☐

Engaged in pleasurable activities and hobbies ☐

Sought meaning and purpose in my life ☐

RELATIONAL CARE

Told people close to me why they were important ☐

Established or maintained healthy limits when necessary ☐

Let go of being "right" ☐

Took a nonjudgmental stance toward others ☐

Practiced empathy ☐

Spent time with people I care about ☐

SPIRITUAL CARE

Attended religious or spiritual services ☐

Spent time with others who have similar beliefs and goals ☐

Practiced mindfulness or meditated ☐

Prayed or asked others to pray for me ☐

Read or watched things that inspire me ☐

Honored my own values ☐

THIS WEEK...

I CREATED MORE HAPPINESS IN MY LIFE BY

I AM MOST THANKFUL FOR

I FOUND PEACE OF MIND IN

MONTHLY

SELF-CARE ASSESSMENT

Over the past 28 days, how often have you engaged in these specific self-care methods?

SCORING	
4	**Always**
3	**Often**
2	**Sometimes**
1	**Rarely**
0	Not applicable to me at this time

PHYSICAL CARE	SCORE
Exercised 4-6 times a week	
Balanced sleep	
Paid attention to nutrition	
Ate mindfully	
Used alcohol in moderation	
Did not self-medicate	

TOTAL SCORE FOR THIS SECTION

EMOTIONAL CARE	SCORE
Asked for help	
Went to individual or family therapy	
Made time for enjoyable activities	
Practiced self-compassion	
Engaged in pleasurable activities and hobbies	
Sought meaning and purpose in my life	

TOTAL SCORE FOR THIS SECTION

TOTAL SCORE PER SECTION

20-24	**Excellent!** You're doing a great job of taking care of yourself in this area.
15-19	**Very good.** Identify and address any gaps in self-care.
BELOW 15	**No one is perfect.** Is this an area of growth for you?

Remember, a score of zero (not applicable) in any area may lower your section score.

RELATIONAL CARE	SCORE
Told people close to me why they were important	
Established or maintained healthy limits when necessary	
Let go of being "right"	
Took a nonjudgmental stance toward others	
Practiced empathy	
Spent time with people I care about	

TOTAL SCORE FOR THIS SECTION

SPIRITUAL CARE	SCORE
Attended religious or spiritual services	
Spent time with others who have similar beliefs and goals	
Practiced mindfulness or meditated	
Prayed or asked others to pray for me	
Read or watched things that inspire me	
Honored my own values	

TOTAL SCORE FOR THIS SECTION

HOW TO HAVE A TOUGH CONVERSATION

I get a lot of questions about when and how to talk about the hard stuff. These are topics that potentially bring up a lot of shame, feelings of rejection, or perhaps they may be a reminder of a loss.

Lengthy conversations often get tuned out or you might risk being ignored if the message is too long. When in doubt, decide to have shorter, more concise conversations. You can always add more details or information at a later time.

I have some ideas that would have been helpful for my family members, and I'm wondering if they might be something that you could also try.

1. KEEP CONVERSATIONS SHORT

Use a format to ask for something or say no and stick to "I" statements) instead of starting out a conversation with the word "you"). Discussions don't have to be long or drawn out.

It might be tempting to play the family historian and talk about everything that's happened over the past year or how a particular behavior impacted the family last month, but you can keep the topic related to just what you need to say at that moment. Your loved one knows what happened last month and likely still feels embarrassed or regretful. They don't need to hear about it one more time unless it's highly relevant to what you need to say today.

2. WAIT UNTIL YOU AND YOUR LOVED ONE ARE RELAXED AND CALM

Sometimes I hear from parents that they don't want to have difficult conversations when their loved one is in a good mood. Often they think that they'll "ruin" the moment, but it's better to have these conversations when everyone is feeling relatively relaxed and calm.

Do challenging topics sometimes interfere with a good day? Absolutely; but difficult conversations are even harder when people are upset, angry, sad, or feeling a lot of shame.

Often conversations can go surprisingly well when everyone is feeling relatively secure.

3. IF YOU CANNOT SPEAK, WRITE

If you suspect that your family member, friend, or loved one will do something similar to what I did and shut down or run away when difficult topics come up, you could always try writing a letter, email, or just send a text.

At one time I was working with parents who wanted to address their adolescent son's hygiene, but they believed that the conversation would trigger a lot of shame for him. I suggested that the mom text her son and gently remind him that he needed to schedule enough time to take a shower before the family went to a cousin's birthday party later that day.

Much to everyone's surprise (including mine!), the idea worked, and there were no meltdowns over what had been a sensitive issue in the past.

FOR THIS WEEK

What does your loved one do when difficult topics come up?

Do they hide, shut down, or attack?

What has been the most helpful way for you to talk about the things no one wants to address?

CHECKLIST

Check all that you accomplished
(or plan to accomplish) this week.

PHYSICAL CARE

Exercised 4–6 times ☐

Balanced sleep ☐

Paid attention to nutrition ☐

Ate mindfully ☐

Used alcohol in moderation ☐

Did not self-medicate ☐

EMOTIONAL CARE

Asked for help ☐

Went to individual or family therapy ☐

Made time for enjoyable activities ☐

Practiced self-compassion ☐

Engaged in pleasurable activities and hobbies ☐

Sought meaning and purpose in my life ☐

RELATIONAL CARE

Told people close to me why they were important ☐

Established or maintained healthy limits when necessary ☐

Let go of being "right" ☐

Took a nonjudgmental stance toward others ☐

Practiced empathy ☐

Spent time with people I care about ☐

SPIRITUAL CARE

Attended religious or spiritual services ☐

Spent time with others who have similar beliefs and goals ☐

Practiced mindfulness or meditated ☐

Prayed or asked others to pray for me ☐

Read or watched things that inspire me ☐

Honored my own values ☐

THIS WEEK...

I CREATED MORE
HAPPINESS IN MY LIFE BY

I AM MOST
THANKFUL FOR

I FOUND PEACE
OF MIND IN

WEEK 50

THEIR HAPPINESS

A wise mom once shared with me, "I'm not responsible for my son's happiness." And, of course, she's right. No one can be entirely responsible for another person's health and happiness.

However, there was a time in my own life when I believed with all my heart that other people were responsible for almost every aspect of my life. I saw myself as a victim, and if I felt hopeless or suicidal, someone wasn't doing something right. If I felt scared, someone had to drop everything and comfort me.

For way too many years, it made sense to me to blame someone or demand that the nearest person "fix" whatever crisis I had created. If they didn't jump quickly enough, then that was even more evidence that I was unwanted and unloved.

It wasn't until I took part in a DBT program that I learned that there were things I could do all on my own to increase my sense of well-being and self-worth. If I didn't like how I was feeling at that moment, I now had the freedom to take action in the form of DBT skills and turn my emotions and thoughts around ever so slightly. It wasn't perfect (it still isn't), but it was life-changing.

THAT GIFT OF EMPOWERMENT WAS ONE OF THE GREATEST THINGS THAT DBT GAVE ME.

Today I can take responsibility for many areas throughout my life. I am responsible for my income, how I manage my day, how clean I keep my car, who I spend time with, who I consult with when I have a problem I cannot quickly solve, and what skills I use throughout the day. Instead of being a burden, these responsibilities now add to my happiness and emotional health. They provide meaning and purpose.

Your family member or loved one probably isn't all that different from me. Instead of absolving them from the responsibilities of daily life, perhaps they are ready to take those next brave steps toward adulthood.

FOR THIS WEEK

Where is your loved one regarding their emotional development?

Are you helping or hindering your family member's necessary steps for growing up?

Could adding more responsibility to their lives also increase their happiness?

CHECKLIST

Check all that you accomplished
(or plan to accomplish) this week.

PHYSICAL CARE

Exercised 4-6 times ☐

Balanced sleep ☐

Paid attention to nutrition ☐

Ate mindfully ☐

Used alcohol in moderation ☐

Did not self-medicate ☐

EMOTIONAL CARE

Asked for help ☐

Went to individual or family therapy ☐

Made time for enjoyable activities ☐

Practiced self-compassion ☐

Engaged in pleasurable activities and hobbies ☐

Sought meaning and purpose in my life ☐

RELATIONAL CARE

Told people close to me why they were important ☐

Established or maintained healthy limits when necessary ☐

Let go of being "right" ☐

Took a nonjudgmental stance toward others ☐

Practiced empathy ☐

Spent time with people I care about ☐

SPIRITUAL CARE

Attended religious or spiritual services ☐

Spent time with others who have similar beliefs and goals ☐

Practiced mindfulness or meditated ☐

Prayed or asked others to pray for me ☐

Read or watched things that inspire me ☐

Honored my own values ☐

THIS WEEK...

I CREATED MORE
HAPPINESS IN MY LIFE BY

I AM MOST
THANKFUL FOR

I FOUND PEACE
OF MIND IN

25 BEHAVIORS TO REWARD

Whether you like it or not, you're in an important position of being a role model, cheerleader, and potentially a reinforcer of behaviors that will help your loved one recover and have a happier and healthier future.

I often hear from frustrated family members and friends who will ask me something like, "Doesn't she know how hurtful it is when she's in the middle of a rage and tells me that she hates me? She's so dismissive once the episode has passed."

There's frequently a significant disconnect between our experiences and having an understanding of those experiences. People with BPD may see things very differently.

Because your family member may not always know exactly what behaviors you expect, you may need to reward them for the times when they:

1. Ask for help before things become a crisis or emergency
2. Ask for help in a way that is respectful and kind
3. Show empathy towards others
4. Practice forgiveness
5. Use good boundaries with friends and family members
6. Remember to say "please" and "thank you"
7. Take time to understand someone else's point of view
8. Refrain from being judgmental
9. Are on time for appointments
10. Engage in philanthropic activities or volunteerism
11. Recognize that we are using a DBT skill
12. Make good decisions about self-care (such as going to bed at a reasonable hour)
13. Help others without expecting anything in return
14. Share
15. Refrain from blaming
16. Think about the consequences of our behavior
17. Show appropriate emotional restraint in public
18. Accurately validate their own thoughts, emotions, and experiences
19. Do the right thing instead of the easy thing
20. Are transparent and vulnerable without revealing too much information
21. Set aside a little savings for emergencies or unexpected expenses
22. Are proactive in problem-solving
23. Seek work or take an interest in returning to school
24. Express appreciation or gratitude
25. Refrain from being (re)victimized

Now a reward from you can be anything from a short written thank you note or text to saying something in person like:

"It would have been easier to leave the dishes in your room. Thank you for taking a moment to bring them into the kitchen. I really appreciate it."

"It meant a lot to me that you were ready on time. I don't like how I sound when I'm nagging."

"I know that this was a difficult conversation to have. I'm glad that we were able to be honest with each other about what's been happening between us over the last few days."

"That store clerk was rude to us. You were so skillful in how you handled the situation."

"I screwed up earlier by shouting. Thank you for forgiving me when I'm not as skillful as I can be."

"You seem happier now that you're volunteering at the animal shelter a couple of days a week. It makes me glad to see you smiling more."

FOR THIS WEEK

Notice one of the behaviors (or variations of the behaviors) listed and then reward your family member or friend by drawing attention to it in a positive way.

CHECKLIST

Check all that you accomplished (or plan to accomplish) this week.

PHYSICAL CARE

Exercised 4-6 times ☐

Balanced sleep ☐

Paid attention to nutrition ☐

Ate mindfully ☐

Used alcohol in moderation ☐

Did not self-medicate ☐

EMOTIONAL CARE

Asked for help ☐

Went to individual or family therapy ☐

Made time for enjoyable activities ☐

Practiced self-compassion ☐

Engaged in pleasurable activities and hobbies ☐

Sought meaning and purpose in my life ☐

RELATIONAL CARE

Told people close to me why they were important ☐

Established or maintained healthy limits when necessary ☐

Let go of being "right" ☐

Took a nonjudgmental stance toward others ☐

Practiced empathy ☐

Spent time with people I care about ☐

SPIRITUAL CARE

Attended religious or spiritual services ☐

Spent time with others who have similar beliefs and goals ☐

Practiced mindfulness or meditated ☐

Prayed or asked others to pray for me ☐

Read or watched things that inspire me ☐

Honored my own values ☐

THIS WEEK...

I CREATED MORE HAPPINESS IN MY LIFE BY

I AM MOST THANKFUL FOR

I FOUND PEACE OF MIND IN

YOUR YEAR IN REVIEW

You did it! You made it this far. I hope that you're in a healthier and happier place than when you started this book 52 weeks ago. It's time for an inventory about what went right this past year. Now is not the time to focus on past mistakes, remember how others hurt us, or think about the things we wish we had done differently. **Please focus on your successes.**

This week I'd love for you to take a few minutes to understand your family member's best moments. I've come up with a list of open-ended statements for you to explore.

YOU CAN PICK A FEW THAT APPLY TO YOU AND YOUR SITUATION:

My loved one was happiest this past year when they...

My loved one felt most confident when they were engaged in...

My loved one made the most progress when they...

My loved one would say that their best moment this past year was when...

My loved one felt most secure when...

My loved one felt most hopeful when...

My loved one felt most understood when...

My loved one was most trusting when...

My loved one learned a valuable lesson when...

The one thing that seemed to make the most significant difference this past year was...

AND THEN I'D LOVE TO SEE YOU APPLY SOME SIMILAR QUESTIONS FOR YOURSELF IN YOUR RELATIONSHIP:

I was happiest this past year when I...

I felt most confident when I was engaged in...

I made the most progress when I...

I would say that my best moment this past year was when I...

I felt most secure when...

I felt most hopeful when...

I felt most understood when...

I was most trusting when...

I learned a valuable lesson when...

The one thing that seemed to make the most significant difference this past year for me was...

FOR THIS WEEK

This is not an exercise that will take
5 or 10 minutes.

Please set aside at least 30 quiet minutes to
begin to think about and journal your answers.

CHECKLIST

Check all that you accomplished
(or plan to accomplish) this week.

PHYSICAL CARE

Exercised 4-6 times ☐

Balanced sleep ☐

Paid attention to nutrition ☐

Ate mindfully ☐

Used alcohol in moderation ☐

Did not self-medicate ☐

EMOTIONAL CARE

Asked for help ☐

Went to individual or family therapy ☐

Made time for enjoyable activities ☐

Practiced self-compassion ☐

Engaged in pleasurable activities and hobbies ☐

Sought meaning and purpose in my life ☐

RELATIONAL CARE

Told people close to me why they were important ☐

Established or maintained healthy limits when necessary ☐

Let go of being "right" ☐

Took a nonjudgmental stance toward others ☐

Practiced empathy ☐

Spent time with people I care about ☐

SPIRITUAL CARE

Attended religious or spiritual services ☐

Spent time with others who have similar beliefs and goals ☐

Practiced mindfulness or meditated ☐

Prayed or asked others to pray for me ☐

Read or watched things that inspire me ☐

Honored my own values ☐

THIS WEEK...

**I CREATED MORE
HAPPINESS IN MY LIFE BY**

**I AM MOST
THANKFUL FOR**

**I FOUND PEACE
OF MIND IN**

MONTHLY

SELF-CARE ASSESSMENT

Over the past 28 days, how often have you engaged in these specific self-care methods?

PHYSICAL CARE	SCORE
Exercised 4–6 times a week	
Balanced sleep	
Paid attention to nutrition	
Ate mindfully	
Used alcohol in moderation	
Did not self-medicate	

TOTAL SCORE FOR THIS SECTION

EMOTIONAL CARE	SCORE
Asked for help	
Went to individual or family therapy	
Made time for enjoyable activities	
Practiced self-compassion	
Engaged in pleasurable activities and hobbies	
Sought meaning and purpose in my life	

TOTAL SCORE FOR THIS SECTION

TOTAL SCORE PER SECTION

20-24	**Excellent!** You're doing a great job of taking care of yourself in this area.
15-19	**Very good.** Identify and address any gaps in self-care.
BELOW 15	**No one is perfect.** Is this an area of growth for you?

Remember, a score of zero (not applicable) in any area may lower your section score.

RELATIONAL CARE	SCORE
Told people close to me why they were important	
Established or maintained healthy limits when necessary	
Let go of being "right"	
Took a nonjudgmental stance toward others	
Practiced empathy	
Spent time with people I care about	

TOTAL SCORE FOR THIS SECTION

SPIRITUAL CARE	SCORE
Attended religious or spiritual services	
Spent time with others who have similar beliefs and goals	
Practiced mindfulness or meditated	
Prayed or asked others to pray for me	
Read or watched things that inspire me	
Honored my own values	

TOTAL SCORE FOR THIS SECTION

RECOMMENDED BOOKS AND WEBSITES

CRISIS/ EMOTIONAL SUPPORT

7 Cups of Tea
7cupsoftea.com

Befrienders
befrienders.org

IMAlive
imalive.org

Lifeline Crisis Chat
crisischat.org

National Suicide Prevention Lifeline
1-800-273-8255
suicidepreventionlifeline.org

RAINN
rainn.org

Samaritans
samaritans.org

Unsuicide
unsuicide.wikispaces.com

My local crisis line, peer support organization, or sponsor:

_____

_____

_____

_____

_____

ORGANIZATIONS

Active Minds
activeminds.org

Clubhouse International
clubhouse-intl.org

Depression and Bipolar Support Alliance
dbsalliance.org

Mind
mind.org.uk

National Alliance on Mental Illness
nami.org

National Education Alliance for Borderline Personality Disorder
borderlinepersonalitydisorder.com

NEDA
nationaleatingdisorders.org

Recovery International
recoveryinternational.org

SMART Recovery
smartrecovery.org

DIALECTICAL BEHAVIOR THERAPY

Behavioral Tech
behavioraltech.org

Linehan Institute
linehaninstitute.org

My Dialectical Life
mydialecticallife.com

Now Matters Now
nowmattersnow.org

BOOKS

Aguirre, B. & Galen, G. (2015).
Coping with BPD:
DBT and CBT skills to soothe the symptoms of borderline personality disorder
Oakland, CA: New Harbinger Publications.

Aguirre, B. & Galen, G. (2013).
Mindfulness for borderline personality disorder:
Relieve your suffering using the core skill of Dialectical Behavior Therapy.
Oakland, CA: New Harbinger Publications.

Blauner, S. R. (2003).
How I stayed alive when my brain was trying to kill me:
One person's guide to suicide prevention.
New York, NY: HarperCollins.

Brach, T. (2004).
Radical acceptance: Embracing your life with the heart of a Buddha.
New York, NY: Bantam Books.

Corso, D. (2017).
Stronger than BPD: The girl's guide to taking control of
intense emotions, drama and chaos using DBT.
Oakland, CA: New Harbinger Publications.

Frankl, V. E. (2006).
Man's search for meaning.
Boston, MA: Beacon Press.

Fruzzetti, A. E. (2004).
The high-conflict couple:
A DBT guide to finding peace, intimacy, and validation.
Oakland, CA: New Harbinger Publications.

Germer, C. K. (2009).
The mindful path to self-compassion:
Freeing yourself from destructive thoughts and emotions.
New York, NY: Guilford Press.

Gunderson, J. & Hoffman, P. (Eds.). (2016).
Beyond borderline: True stories of recovery from borderline personality disorder.
Oakland, CA: New Harbinger Publications.

Gunderson, J. & Hoffman, P. (Eds.). (2005).
Understanding and treating borderline personality disorder:
A guide for professionals and families.
Washington, DC: American Psychiatric Association Publishing.

Hall, K. D. (2014).
The emotionally sensitive person:
Finding peace when your emotions overwhelm you.
Oakland, CA: New Harbinger Publications.

Kabat-Zinn, J. (2013).
Full catastrophe living:
Using the wisdom of your body and mind to face stress, pain, and illness.
New York, NY: Bantam.

Kabat-Zinn, J. (1994).
Wherever you go, there you are: Mindfulness meditation for everyday life.
New York, NY: Hyperion.

Linehan, M. M. (1993).
Cognitive-Behavioral Treatment of Borderline Personality Disorder.
New York, NY: The Guilford Press.

Linehan, M. M. (2014).
DBT skills training handouts and worksheets. Second edition.
New York, NY: The Guilford Press.

Linehan, M. M. (2014).
DBT skills training manual. Second edition.
New York, NY: The Guilford Press.

Manning, S. Y. (2011).
Loving someone with borderline personality disorder:
How to keep out-of-control emotions from destroying your relationship.
New York, NY: The Guilford Press.

Taitz, J. (2012).
End emotional eating: Using DBT skills to cope with difficult emotions
and develop a healthy relationship with food.
Oakland, CA: New Harbinger Publications.

ABOUT THE AUTHOR

Amanda L. Smith, LCSW, is founder of Hope for BPD where she provides treatment consultation and referrals for family members located throughout the United States.

Her career in mental health began when she served as the executive director of the Pinellas County, Florida affiliate of the National Alliance for Mental Illness (NAMI).

In 2007, she founded Florida BPD Association—a 501(c)(3) organization dedicated to providing advocacy, education, and support for persons diagnosed with BPD and their families.

Amanda received her MSW at Baylor University and is currently working as a DBT therapist in Waco, Texas.

Her website is **www.HopeForBPD.com**

MORE FROM THE BPD WELLNESS SERIES

The *Dialectical Behavior Therapy Wellness Planner* is a helpful tool for anyone who struggles with emotional sensitivity and/or Borderline Personality Disorder to use as you work toward creating a healthier, more meaningful life—a life worth living—by balancing acceptance and change. Use it to help manage anxiety, maintain sobriety, or just keep your life in better balance.

The Big Book on Borderline Personality Disorder gives you the information and tools to reclaim your life. With warmth and humor, Shehrina Rooney shows you how you can find contentment, stability, and the freedom to enjoy each day as it comes.

Contrary to popular belief, BPD is not a life sentence.

Available at **www.unhookedbooks.com** and bookstores everywhere.